CHERISHABLE
LOVE and MARRIAGE

CHERISHABLE
LOVE and MARRIAGE

David Augsburger

HERALD PRESS
Scottdale, Pennsylvania
Kitchener, Ontario

All Scripture quotations, unless otherwise indicated, are from
The New Testament in Modern English, © J. B. Phillips, 1958.
Used by permission of The Macmillan Company.

Preface

"Cherishable." Say that as you think of your wife, your husband, your marriage. What do you experience?

"I will love and cherish," you once said in public contract. You've "loved." Have you learned to "cherish"?

To cherish, is to see the preciousness of another, to prize that preciousness. It is a drive toward relatedness and intimacy that is present in each of us. For some persons it goes unrecognized and unsatisfied. But as we become aware of what we truly want and need, we begin to find and know each other.

I want to acknowledge the valuable criticism and suggestions of Daniel Heinrichs, MD, Jim Gaede, George Konrad, Clyde Weaver, and Bernie Wiebe from their broad experience in individual and family therapy, and to James Fairfield for his editorial assistance.

Obviously, much of *Cherishable* comes from the life Nancy and I are finding together. We would like you to believe that only the best emotions and interchanges are true of us, but the truth is, we've experienced both sides of each other, and we've found that anger and love, conflict and conciliation, distance and intimacy can be equally cherishable.

— David Augsburger
December, 1972

Contents

"I
WILL
LOVE
AND
CHERISH"

LOVE
LIVES
WHEN
CHERISHED,
WHEN
NOURISHED
FAITHFULLY

SO
IT
ALSO IS
WITH MARRIAGE.
PERISHABLE
BUT
CHERISHABLE.

CHAPTER ONE

Marriage Means . . .

1930

MARRIAGE:
Like Flies On A Windowpane,
Those In Want Out,
Those Out Want In.

1960

CAUTION:
Marriage May Be Hazardous
To Your Health.

1980

This Marriage License
Valid Only For 90 Days.
Renewable Only Upon Consent
Of Both Parties
For a Period Of Two Years.

2010

Marriage / 'marij / n [old English, now obsolete] a: a contract between a man and a woman called respectively husband and wife. b: a special kind of social order for the founding and maintaining of a family, practiced from prehistoric times to the last of the twentieth century. c: occurs now only among primitive cultures and in ethnic or religious subgroups in isolated locations.

o   o   o

Is marriage approaching obsolescence?

As human relationships adapt to the changing patterns of life in a highly mobile age, will the family disappear? Will marriage pass into extinction?

Some suggest that it should, at least, undergo major alteration.

"Marriage is the only human contract in the Western Christian world that has no time length, no opportunity for review, and no socially acceptable means of termination," Mrs. Virginia Satir, Esalen Institute, Big Sur, California, told a national meeting of the American Psychological Association. She recommended an "apprentice period" for people contemplating marriage, a five-year terminal point for all marriages with the option of either renewal or cancellation of the contract, and specially trained, government financed substitute parents for the children involved in dissolved marriages. [1]

"I, John, take thee, Mary — for the next five years." Is that the flexible, easily alterable kind of contract that will shape man-woman relationships in the next century?

Or will marriage become a "nonlegal, voluntary association," as some psychologists recommend, to free the participants from "unnecessary guilt and unresolvable snarls of responsibility"?

Or will marriage be socially recognized on various levels

of responsibility and privilege? Such as the two-level system advocated by many who hope to protect the integrity of the family as a permanent, indissoluble unit for the rearing of children.

Purpose of this two-level marriage system: to provide time to build a husband-wife relationship before children are permitted.

License: first level. Five years cohabitation, divorce allowed. No children permitted. Then application may be filed to move up to . . .

License: second level. Permanent marriage. No divorce permitted. Children allowed. This level, exclusive, permanent, and indissoluble, would be available only to selected couples. The first level would be for the bulk of humans who prefer more flexibility, greater variety, and less commitment to responsibility.

Whatever the new shapes of marriage will be, they will not likely be formed from the visions of theorists, or framed by social architects turned legislators. As in the past, the forms will likely emerge from the values and practices of people in general who express in life the meaning — or the absence of meaning — in marriage. It is they who are debating it.

o   o   o

"Honored judges.

"Worthy opponents.

"Ladies and gentlemen.

"In this debate be it resolved that: Marriage means the denial of personal freedom, the loss of voluntary love, the end of meaningful living."

Would you care to debate that common proposition and present a case for marriage? Let's hear the opposing point of view.

"Marriage is a senseless surrender of personal freedom.

It demands that both parties sign away their future. A future neither can foresee. A future that can totally change their values, may utterly alter their interests, and will likely diminish their attraction to each other."

Certainly you must concede that the future is all unknown, but that argument works for both sides. Perhaps it will bring deep intimacy, profound understanding, and enriching relationships.

"Marriage is a tragic loss of voluntary love. If any love at all survives the passing of the first flush of romance, it is a forced love, wrung from the partners by the pressures of long-dead promises."

Or can a promise of love be a living, breathing thing which renewed every day is new every day in a loving, voluntary way?

"Marriage is the end of meaningful living. When persons are no longer free to give love because they want to give love and for no other reason, then the spark of joy is out!"

No man sells his soul in marriage; no woman signs away her integrity as a person. They continue to possess and exercise their privileges of choice. They give themselves to each other from day to day because that is the way of unconditional love.

o   o   o

Marriage, love, commitment — what fascinating matters to debate!

Choose your proposition. Present your case.

"Resolved: Love is only love when it lives in absolute freedom to give or to withhold itself from moment to moment. No precedent can bind it. The past and its promises have no power to bind."

Or is that . . . "Love me my way today, or no way tomorrow."

"Resolved: Love is truly love when it rises spontaneously as an affectionate response to another's attractiveness."

Or is that only admiration? Is not love still love even when it rises in spontaneous anger at the loved one's obstinacy?

"Resolved: Love is only love when it offers itself in total fidelity, unafraid of the future."

Or is unconditional faithfulness too much to ask of the fickle human heart?

o   o   o

HE: Understand, darling, our love is much too beautiful for us to spoil it by red-taping ourselves together with legal papers.

SHE: You mean a license? Vows to each other?

HE: I mean no license or marriage! I think love should unite us. Love that is free and voluntary.

SHE: And that means no marriage, right? Nothing I can hang on to?

HE: You could hang on to love. Our love is a unity of our own making, and this way it wouldn't be just "some ink that has dried upon some lines."

SHE: You mean that we'll always love each other then, because we want to, and not because we have to?

HE: Uh-huh, you've got the idea, Baby.

SHE: But why can't you promise me that you'll always love me, no matter what?

HE: I do . . . you know that. . . .

SHE: And why not tell the world that it's true?

HE: I will . . . of course, I will. . . .

SHE: So what's wrong with making it a contract?

HE: Darling, I don't think you understand. You see, I don't want to stay with you because I have to, but because I want to. . . .

SHE: And what happens if you stop wanting to?

HE: You wouldn't want me to stay on just because of a

license, would you?

SHE: So I wake up some morning and you're gone? Then what do I have?

HE: You can trust me, can't you?

SHE: Yes, I trust you. I trust you enough to promise myself to you for always, like forever . . . and even on paper.

HE: If you trusted me, you'd give yourself to me without the security of a paper marriage. That's really an act of love and faith! To give yourself to someone you love without all that legal stuff. Sure it takes guts, but that's the risk of love.

SHE: But dearest, doesn't it take even more courage to promise yourself to another forever — handing over yourself, your hopes, your future? Even though the other person is still pretty much a stranger to you? Yet you offer everything to him?

HE: You mean in marriage?

SHE: Yes, in marriage. With a contract!

o   o   o

"Should we not refuse this ink-stains-dried-on-dotted-lines view of marriage," some suggest, "and let common law be the honest expression of sharing a common life-in-love?"

Is a marriage contract a cop-out on living courageously? A cheap bargain struck for security? Is it less romantic, less exciting, less demanding than a love-liaison that lives from day to day? Or is a contractual marriage a more bold and risky surrender of self and future, more bold than any private agreement which can be dissolved if distance develops between the two? True, to risk deep involvement with no public pledge of security to guarantee unconditional faithfulness demands a gutsy bravado, an act of faith.

But handing over your hopes, your future, your dreams to someone you love enough to give an irrevocable pledge of fidelity demands even more faith. To commit yourself to another person who remains greatly a stranger to you — is an act of faith. To commit yourself, knowing that stranger will undergo great change — change to be surpassed only, perhaps, by your own — is an even greater act of faith.

Is a marriage contract a blindly irresponsible promissory note written on the future? Is it a pledging of irrevocable fidelity in a future you cannot imagine, of a future self you cannot predict, to a future person you may not understand or want to understand?

"Marriage means coming to reality some dreary morning and finding yourself thirtyish, firmly set in life, and tied to some undesirable person, selected by some ignorant eighteen-year-old kid on a dark night in a parked car by a value system you now scorn."

True, but only if the two grow as isolated individuals, each finding his and her own way in life! But that is not what marriage promises to those who enter it, or what those who enter promise. Marriage, mutually shared, is a joint pilgrimage of growing and maturing in which two persons assist each other in exploring and realizing the fullest potential of each.

Is marriage a private action of two persons in love, or a public act of two pledging a contract? Neither. It is something other. Very much other!

Basically, the Christian view of marriage is not that it is primarily or even essentially a binding legal and social contract. The Christian understands marriage as a covenant made under God and in the presence of fellow members of the Christian family. Such a pledge endures, not because of the force of law or the fear of its sanctions, but because an unconditional covenant has been made. A covenant more solemn, more binding, more permanent than any legal contract.

Those who pledge such a covenant before God hold that God Himself has been called a witness to their act, God Himself has joined them together, and "what God has joined together, they will not let man put asunder." This is not to say that such covenants are never violated, can never collapse, and will never be broken. They can and are, else God would not have issued the warning, "Let not man put asunder." But those who commit themselves in awareness of the eternal witness recognize the open-ended promise to be faithful as long as life allows.

Those who pledge such a vow under God and before their fellow sons of God call their brothers and sisters to witness the solemnity and integrity of their act, and by this action they accept the responsibility of living as husband and wife in the larger family of God. Those who stand at attention pledge as witnesses to protect the sanctity of that marriage that no man — either within the circle of brothers or without that circle — shall cut apart what is permanently fused.

Jesus put it in perfect perspective by quoting the oldest document known on the history of marriage, the Book of Genesis, which gives the account of the original instituting of marriage:

But from the beginning of creation, "God made them male and female. For this reason a man shall leave his father and mother and be joined to his wife, and the two shall become one." So they are no longer two but one. What therefore God has joined together, let not man put asunder (Mk. 10:6-9; RSV).

• • •

SHE: Jerry....

HE: Huh?

SHE: Why did you marry me, anyway?

HE: What do you mean by that tone of voice? It was love. You know that, don't you?

SHE: I'm not sure. Did you really love *me*? Or did you....

16

HE: Did I love your body? Not until after I married you. Remember, you wouldn't let me before. . . .

SHE: Oh, stop spoofing me. . . .

HE: Well, what do you expect me to do?

SHE: You could answer me seriously.

HE: Like what?

SHE: Like . . . did you marry me to be really, ʋʰ . . . close? Or just to be comfortable.

HE: Comfortable?

SHE: Yes . . . you know — housekeeping, home cooking, sex twice a week. . . .

HE: Three times.

SHE: Oh, I give up. You won't talk sense. . .

HE: OK . . . OK . . . my answer is "yes."

SHE: Yes?

HE: Yes to both — I married you for closeness and — what'd you say — comfort?

SHE: That's not good enough I want to know why — really why.

HE: You do, uh? And do you want me sniffing through your imaginary motives, too? Did you marry me to get out of nursing the three-to-eleven shift so you wouldn't spend the rest of your life panhandling? Or did you marry me because I looked like a decent catch and that gave you status — or security? Or did you need somebody to lean on? . . .

SHE: You can stop. You're too good at this game.

HE: Game? It's too serious to be called a game.

SHE: What's wrong with figuring out why?

HE: Because you can't. Because it's dangerous. Because it doesn't help to know anyway.

SHE: Yes, it does. If you know what pulled you together, you can build on it if it's good.

HE: Or you could just ask, "What would make our marriage more meaningful?" and then work at it.

SHE: But I can still ask myself "why," can't I?

HE: Sure. No harm in that as long as we're still looking for better and better reasons for loving each other.

SHE: Ummm . . . instead of trying to figure each other out?

HE: Umhum! I'd rather tell you "why" I love you now.

SHE: I guess those are the "whys" that matter, uh?

HE: Mmm!

º   º   º

Why should any two people — as different as people are — care to commit themselves to such a venture as marriage? What could be worth all the difficulties involved in blending two continuingly developing personalities into a unity? What good could possibly justify the enormous energy demanded in achieving and sustaining emotional intimacy, intellectual integrity and social-spiritual-physical fidelity for a half-century of marriage?

Why marry? To regulate and legitimize sexual activities? Sex, within the security and open intimacy of marriage, does find the perfect context for genuinely free love. Then the person experiencing the I-accept-you-completely-as-you-are-and-as-you-will-be kind of love can afford to express himself/herself without any inhibiting fear or rejection. Sex is so bad outside marriage because it is so good inside marriage. But sex is neither the sole nor the central reason for marriage, fascinating and fulfilling as it can be.

Why then marry? For parenthood, repopulation, and continuation of your own bloodlines? Or the extension of your personal or familial ego into the next generation? Parenthood is no longer necessary nor wise for every individual. For many, who are unwilling to give the time and the love needed for maturing of children, it is clearly inadvisable.

Why marry? For social relationships? For community acceptance? Marriage has been virtually a membership card to our social structures. Our community systems have an unspoken prejudice against singles. The unadmitted assumption is that every red-blooded adult ought to indulge in it. It's a base to be touched in life or you're counted out. But one can be *for* marriage without insisting that it is *for* everyone. There is the alternative — and an honorable one — of remaining single. The unmarried state is not a condition to be pitied, or a challenge to matchmakers, or a plight for humorous labeling or libeling. It, too, is a role of dignity.

Why marry? The list of reasons unconfessed but all too real is embarrassingly close to each of us. For her, marriage may be a symbol of success, to prove how desirable, how attractive, how sexually irresistible she is. Or it may be a way of dropping out of competitive work, of copping out on an ill-fitting career, or of seeking an emotionally supportive situation where it may be easier to cope. For him, marriage can mean mistress, laundress, hostess, chef, housekeeper, nanny, nurse, and an all-purpose person to be used as needed.

Many of these reasons, once accepted grudgingly, are thoroughly resented today. Lids are being lifted, motives inspected, assumptions questioned. Well and good! Marriage stands to benefit.

If singleness comes to be respected as a normal and desirable state for persons suited to solitary existence, then marriage may be reserved for persons who live well in intimate and open relationships. (One way to deal with divorce may be to raise the entrance requirements for marriage. The chief cause of divorce, as one wag put it, is marriage.)

If marriage comes to be respected as the truly voluntary decision to live life in an intimate, permanent relationship, then it may become again the act of freedom it was intended to be when "two choose to become one." That's the "why" in answer to the query "why marry?"

19

CHAPTER TWO

To Be Man Means . . .

"It's a heavy burden to bear — perfection."

(Not my wife's perfection, of course, but mine.)

You see, I have to live with myself, and it's not easy, seeing as I'm a perfect husband and father.

It is a bit difficult to make no mistakes, and doubly so when those you love have habitual shortcomings. Yet I have no choice but to go my flawless way.

It is rather embarrassing to be right all the time, and even more so when you are responsible to point out for others where they are wrong. (I'd gladly overlook their mistakes, but being perfect, I have to be totally honest too, you know?)

In fact, it's frustrating to win all the arguments to always have the last word. Naturally my wife can become rather sarcastic, but I accept the situation with great humility. (Being perfect I'm not at all conceited, but that seldom works out to my advantage.)

I'd gladly let my wife win — if it weren't that she's always wrong. If I gave in on the sly to "let her win once in a while" and she later found out how wrong she'd been — pouf — there would go my integrity and her respect.

It's not easy to accept the obligation of being the perfect critic. But since my viewpoints are unbiased by any personal failings, I can offer extremely valuable pointers on living. My wife does find it a bit hard to keep up with the changes I suggest in her. At times she resists them with extreme reluctance, but she usually comes across. Especially when I point out how those same characteristics have gone to seed in her relatives.

My most difficult role? That of judge in settling contested points between the wife and the children. These usually arise the moment I enter the door in the evening. It came as a shock to my wife the first time I was forced to rule against her. But I had no choice. To show the children what justice and perfection is, I need to rule for them and against her 51 percent of the cases. (To prove that marriage hasn't blinded me to my wife's faults.)

It's not an easy life, being perfect. But all in all, I'd much rather have my role than to be one of the ordinary fallible humans that come a dime a dozen. (Although I'm glad I married one of them. We perfect people shouldn't marry among our own kind. It's like incest. And marriages between two of us, when tried, have proven less than successful.) [2]

o   o   o

"Yes, of course there's friction in the family. But it's so unnecessary. We'd have no trouble at all if my wife would just do what I ask her to."

"I told her long ago that three fourths of our problems would be solved if she'd just take my advice without questioning it."

"I don't know why we have these awful arguments. If she'd just listen to reason, they'd never get started. And when we do argue, she won't stay on the issue. She always jumps to criticizing my attitude."

"If she'd just shape up and accept a little of my advice on how to do things better, we could get along great. That is if she'd leave off her infernal nagging."

o   o   o

What makes a husband perfect?

If you found "the perfect husband," he would be the last to believe it. As is the case with any form of maturity, it is not a self-conscious achieving of high goals, but a self-forgetful practice of loving respect that brings human relationships toward perfection.

What then qualifies a husband for a superior rating? If opinion polls could answer that for us, we might quickly eliminate all the shortcomings to which men are prone. Such as this listing of unwanted items:

Question: What makes a man undesirable as a husband and father?

Answer: 1. Lack of understanding of a woman's point of view. 2. Lack of courtesy shown in chivalry and manners. 3. Lack of pride in personal appearance with neatness and "polish." 4. Lack of interest and insight in home relations, child care, and family values. 5. Lack of personal values that put business and success above human relationships. 6. Lack of cooperative attitude toward work around the house and shared family responsibilities.

Question: What makes a man desirable as a husband and father?

Answer: A simple list of the reverse traits to the undesirable characteristics just mentioned? Or do character, integrity, generosity, financial stability, health, intelligence rate higher?

Surprisingly, it is attitudes that consistently come out on the most-wanted listings.

Attitudes like, "He must be companionable — that's giving warm acceptance and showing genuine interest in you." "He should be considerate, I mean place you ahead of other people and other things like job and hobby." "He should be loyal, not just in fidelity where he doesn't let another woman come between you, but also in priorities where he won't let things, finances, and his success come first."

o   o   o

HE: So you want me to know that I don't quite measure up as the ideal husband.

SHE: No, that's not it at all, I was only suggesting. . . .

HE: . . . suggesting that I shape up on your terms?

SHE: Honey . . . listen . . . I only said that I feel sometimes like we married each other for totally different reasons.

HE: Sure, I married you because you're a woman; you married me because I'm a. . . .

SHE: That's not what I mean. I won't judge why you married me. But I expected . . . well, friendship.

HE: Sure, marriage is the most friendly thing a man and a woman can do.

SHE: . . . maybe what I mean is companionship. I guess I expected you to be more companionable.

HE: Companionable? Look, we do all kinds of things together.

SHE: It's not doing things together, it's more like feeling things or thinking things together.

HE: But we don't think about the same kind of things all the time. You think women's things; I think about my work and my interests in politics and the stock market, and all that bores you stiff.

SHE: True, I may not be terribly excited about some of the things you find so fascinating. But I am interested in you and what you're thinking. I'll listen; just try me.

HE: I'm not sure you'd understand it. . . .

SHE: Now that's what I resent. Maybe I am inferior to you educationally, or intellectually, but it sure would feel good if you could at least talk with me like I was an equal.

HE: (Chuckling) Uh-huh! You want me to be dishonest. Is that it?

SHE: Married people can't afford to be perfectly honest.

→ HE: Hold on there. Are you suggesting that it's a good thing to lie to each other?

SHE: I think a husband who won't lie to his wife when love and tact demand it — to bolster her sagging self-confidence — such a man is so low, he's beneath contempt.

HE: That sounds well and good, but who's to decide when it's proper for a husband to lie to please his wife?

SHE: Let her decide, naturally. He can tell when she wants his approval — whether it's deserved or not.

HE: I wouldn't bet on it.

SHE: You would if you knew me better — if we did a little more exploring ideas with each other. Like this. It wasn't so bad, was it?

HE: Of course not, but I'm still hung up on that honesty question.

SHE: Well, maybe it's just where you draw the line between necessary honesty and unnecessary brutality?

HE: Uh-huh! You know, your ideas aren't so bad!

SHE: Yeah? Now was that tact or honesty?

o   o   o

Companionability. Man's most attractive asset to a woman. Yet it's one of the lesser expectations that bring him to marriage.

He expects emotional warmth, particularly to drive out the moody chill that sets in on him when life, work, human relationships, and success aren't coming off on schedule.

He expects emotional sharing in sexual intimacy, in recreational activity, in the pleasures of eating, entertaining, relaxing, in fulfilling the routines of life.

But he doesn't always expect intellectual companionship because he likely continues to find that from the friends, business associates, and other acquaintances (largely male) who provided it before. Those relationships are safer because they can be controlled. And disagreements there can be handled without threatening an ongoing relationship of intimacy.

So it puzzles, and then irritates a man to discover that his wife considers companionship and the communication of ideas, insights, values as supremely important. She assumes the right to know him as an equal, and this grates on any vestigial remains of male superiority. Unless he is willing to at least adapt to her point of view, or, better yet, to adopt it as his own, he will not be a good husband.

Consideration. Man's second most compelling characteristic for building a husband-wife relationship is the ability to see things from her point of view. Actually, it's more of an attitude than an ability. It's an attitude of thoughtful respect coupled with concern.

o   o   o

Live together in harmony,
live together in love,
   as though you had
   only one mind
   and one spirit
      between you.
Never act from motives
of rivalry or personal vanity,

25

but in humility
think more of [one another]
than you do of yourselves.
None of you should think
only of his own affairs,
but [each] should learn
to see things from
other people's point of view.
— Philippians 2:2-4.

Do companionship and considerate mutuality form an inappropriate image for manhood? Or is masculinity inherently "the way of the aggressor"? Is femininity essentially "the way of the victim"? Or do both sexes possess both potentials but in varying amounts? Is there a given-ness in the male and the female with which we must reckon and which we should excuse? Or must both learn to fulfill both roles as the situation affords or demands? Can we excuse the man who chooses the life-style of domination, the pattern of aggressive self-assertion as "making it in a man's world in a man's way"?

Perhaps you may choose to excuse the dominating lifestyle as an appropriate male way to get along in the rough-and-tumble world of business or labor. But in marriage? Does not the man who imposes such a life-style on his wife defeat any and all possibilities of mutual companionship and communication as equal human beings?

"But history demonstrates its practicality, nature proves its inevitability, and God has given man the superior responsibility," say some (male, of course) defenders of male dominance. Does not the Bible teach that the woman must obey her husband? Ephesians 5:22, 1 Peter 3:1.

Three things must be observed on this matter that are usually (in male defensiveness) overlooked.

One: There are no commands for the husband to dominate the wife. Check for yourself Ephesians 5:21-33; Colossians 3:18; 1 Peter 3:1-12. Instead, the command is for the woman to voluntarily place the man first in gentle respect.

Two: There are (not equal, but even more binding) commands to the man to accept his role as husband in the unconditional self-sacrifice of love for the other which Christ Himself demonstrated. Examine Ephesians 5:21-33 again. True, Paul does affirm that the man is "head"; that is, he takes the lead in setting the tone of the relationship. But when Paul describes what the "headship" means, he speaks of self-sacrificing, Christlike love. Headship is then no right for a man to demand, but a right for him to fulfill.

Three: There is no difference between man and woman in acceptance with God now (see Galatians 3:28) and there will be absolutely no difference in their standing before God in eternity — neither male nor female in heaven. Mark 12:18-25. All will be as kings and priests to Him. Revelation 1:6.

Does not this suggest that a man must give up his dominating, aggressive life-style and disavow his self-image of male superiority and supremacy? Does it not indicate that somehow he must adjust his life-style and learn the arts of respecting people as people regardless of their gender, of relating to persons as persons whatever their sex? Does it not demand that he learn a new way of valuing himself, of achieving a self-image as a man?

o   o   o

The male-female difference, however it is defined, is not a matter of inferiority or superiority.

They are equal but not identical. As equal as are an apple and a pear, but they are different to the core. Yet learning from each other, adapting to each other, competing with each other may conceal or even seem to erase these differences. The roles and functions that a husband and wife choose in life may demand and develop the reverse characteristics.

For example, consider these marital partners where the traditional roles are switched: Wife, research chemist; husband, pediatrician. Husband, social worker with a caseload of primary children; wife, shipping clerk in wholesale office supplies. Wife, restaurant manager; husband, chef. You name the combination, the roles can be and are being successfully interchanged.

But is there not an essentially definable something that is uniquely male and female? The classic answer to this is as follows:

The male is essentially the dominating aggressor.

He is the aggressor in sexuality who takes and possesses the woman.

He is the aggressor in business. At its best, this aggression forges progress for the total community. At its lowest, it exploits others, saying: "Someone has to lose so that someone can win; some will have to stay poor so that some of us can be rich."

He is even the aggressor in love, insisting on being the lover who releases the tension of his own stored-up love on the beloved (who may be only a stimulus). So the aggressor prefers loving to being loved. (In some mysterious way, the state of being loved is often intolerable to the aggressive personality.) [3]

There is power, strength, virility, in the way of the aggressor. There is creative drive, and even compassionate action. At its best, that is. At its worst, it is the way of violence and arrogance.

It must be admitted that many male-aggressor-type persons and personalities live in female-type bodies.

The female, in contrast, classically has been considered essentially a submissive victim.

She is the victim who is receptive to the difficulties of life and absorbs its assaults with resignation. This passivity — or receptivity, as it may better be called — is a capacity to absorb suffering and, strangely, find joy in that suffering. It is a capability for accepting drudgery and dullness and finding meaning in that monotony. It absorbs the hurt of the world in the silent wordlessness of feeling, of caring, of taking what is "other" into the self.

There is something redemptive in the way of receptivity. It is the way of forgiving, the way of accepting. It recognizes that truly authentic experience comes through suffering. It cultivates sensitivity, tenderness; it gives dignity and beauty to "feeling." It is willing to accept love and be loved. At its best, that is. At its worst, it becomes a sick passivity which accepts brutality and even sadism wordlessly.

It should also be noted that many receptive-victim-type persons have male-type bodies.

Both the way of the aggressor and the way of the receptor are valuable, and needed. Although each is self-defeating when pursued to the exclusion of the other.

Both ways reach out toward perfection when they are blended with each other in love, and expressed together in loving and being loved.

> Only he who is loved
> And can allow himself to be loved
> Can love and give love.
> Only the loved can be lovers.

Are these the classic distinctions in male and female?

No. Each is a mixture, a blend of both. But each may demonstrate a tendency. In one, toward aggressiveness. In the other, toward receptivity. With that tendency, a greater capacity for its fulfillment is present.

o o o

The female, although by natural inclination a receptor, may turn that quality into a means of aggression. She may consciously seek to compete with and conquer the male in her life, by direct or indirect means, only to find the feminine part of her person becoming angry and frustrated when she achieves her goal of confounding and controlling him. She married a man gentle enough to conquer, then despises him for his inability to oppose her. She attempts to conquer him; in reality, she wants to be defeated, yet insists on having the last word.

The male, although by nature an aggressor, may seek to achieve his ends through submission. Rather than stand up to a dominant wife, he acquiesces to her demands to escape making a scene. He chose a woman strong enough to dominate him (like the mother who conditioned him) yet he despises her for always being victor. So he may strike back at the one vulnerable point where he can get at her essential femaleness — her receptivity. He begins an affair with another. Not for the sake of sex, but to say, "I reject you as a woman; I refuse the femininity you offer to me vaginally when you refuse all other forms of receptivity." Then he hates himself for the weakness shown in his infidelity.

o   o   o

Confusing? Only because persons can be frightfully confused in who and what they are and are meant to become.

Confused we are. Frightfully complex and so unable to sort out our motivations and become the persons we must be if we are to be free. We compound our problems as we twist and turn to escape ourselves and the potentials bound up within us — to be aggressive or recessive.

Neither way is superior nor inferior. Both are indispensable. Both must be exercised in careful respect for each other.

Both must be blended or expressed in complementary

relationship before we achieve true humanity.

Jesus demonstrated both roles in perfect balance. He was the perfect receptor in absorbing the hurts and cares of others into Himself. The way of Jesus was the way of the self-sacrificing, all-atoning, and finally slain Lamb. Yet He also gave perfect expression to the way of the aggressor, as well. He is the Lion who triumphs, defeating evil with courage, with unflinching fidelity to truth, and with the power of love.

He is both Victor and victim. He dies voluntarily even though He does not want to die. Does not Gethsemane show that beyond doubt? He suffers violence and abuse forgivingly even though such force and violence are beneath His contempt.

He brings the two together in perfect balance and harmony. He is what we should begin to be in our own personhood of marriage. Two persons, possessing all the confused potentials of both polarities, can break through to a complementary relationship that frees each to become more than he or she would be alone.

In Christ, male and female find their fullness as two become one in Him.

> Of course, in the sight of God neither "man" nor "woman" has any separate existence. For if woman was made originally for man, no man is now born except by a woman, and both man and woman, like everything else, owe their existence to God (1 Cor. 11:11, 12).

o   o   o

Each person has two major measurements of his own worth: what he is, and what he does.

Most men look at what they do as the first measurement of their personal worth. It's the basis of their self-image, their key to self-understanding and self-respect.

Should what a man does determine what he is? Or

should this come last? (If it doesn't in life, it will in this chapter.)

o   o   o

HE: I was a man, until I got married.

SHE: And what did I make of you?

HE: I don't know. You tied me down, I guess.

SHE: I did what?

HE: I had to take this job. I hate to keep up with the bills. I had to give up all the things I enjoy.

SHE: And I suppose I'm to blame for all that.

HE: Well, it's marriage and the two kids.

SHE: But where would you be if we hadn't married?

HE: Through night school. I'd be a draftsman, not just a parts man in a garage. I'm a nobody.

SHE: You're a somebody to me and the kids.

HE: Yeah? I work all day, come home pooped, watch a little TV, grouch at the kids, then sack out. So that's living? Where's the old spark?

SHE: So why take it out on us?

HE: Because . . . because, what am I? A married man with two kids, a lousy job, no future. It's castrating.

SHE: You really feel that way?

HE: Do I ever! I'm so sick of it all I could. . . .

SHE: But you've got a family that loves you. . . .

HE: Look, that's fine for a woman, but don't woman-talk me. I'm a man, see? I've got to get somewhere, to prove I'm somebody, to get ahead.

SHE: Why can't you relax and enjoy your family? Live a little. . . .

HE: You sit there straight-faced and call this living? I've got to have something more. I'm a man.

SHE: So you're a man.

HE: Don't you understand? If I can't win success on my own terms, I don't want anything. I've got to be my own kind of man, and nothing, nobody, can stop me.

SHE: What are you going to do?

HE: If I knew, I'd already be doing it, wouldn't I?

o   o   o

What is the measure of a man? His job? His skills? The work he can perform? The salary he can command? The influence he can wield? The services he can render? Are any or are all of these combined adequate measurements of manhood? Or are they only utilitarian yardsticks for comparing one man's usefulness against others?

For many men there are no other yardsticks to use in making self-evaluation. Ask them who they are, they respond automatically with their occupation or profession. Ask them how they're doing, they measure progress in promotion or in pay-scale. It is true that work and paycheck are simple, tangible evidences of a man's attempts at living, but they totally ignore the real stuff of life — the relationships.

But how do you measure relationships? By evaluating and ranking the roles a man fills — his work role as an employee, his friendship role with associates, his community role as a citizen, his religious role as a member of a church, his family role as a husband and father? After you've named them all — worker, counselor, listener, citizen, member, provider, lover, confidant, parent, disciplinarian — then how do you stack them up in order of priority?

Most men pass value judgments on their roles unconsciously by naming some of them "things I am" and others "things I do." Which are which for you?

Once when suggesting to a minister friend in difficulty with his family that he might consider scaling his priorities as first, maintaining personal integrity; second, marital intimacy; third, parental responsibility; and fourth, professional proficiency — he rejected those values.

I can't possibly put my profession fourth. It's a part of

33

the first one," he said. "You see, my being a pastor is all bound up in my being a person."

But must I say my profession is what I am and my marriage and my family are only some of the things I do?

Or could we scale our values in terms of their lasting interpersonal significance, placing persons above things, interpersonal relationships above personal achievement, and love above power?

That might bring a man to rate his experiences of being loved and of giving love as the most central measurement of being alive — as a man.

That could bring a man to value his experience of marriage and parenthood as more important than his position or profession — in measuring his manhood.

That may bring a man to put relationships of companionable living, considerate loving, and open communication at the top of his priorities — for masculinity.

o o o

To be a man
  Is to possess the strength to love another
    Not the need to dominate over others.

To be a man
  Is to experience the courage to accept another,
    Not the compulsion to be an aggressor.

To be a man
  Is to keep faith with human values in relationships,
    Not to value oneself by position or possessions.

To be a man
  Is to be free to give love
    And to be free to accept love in return.

CHAPTER THREE

To Be Woman Means . . .

What am I as a woman?

Just a sexual object to be panted after, pursued, taken in conquest, and then ignored? Am I not more than a possessor of erogenous zones?

Just a baby-making machine? Am I not more than an incubator, a wet nurse, a nanny?

Just a second-class citizen, given inferior jobs with discriminating pay scales, unequal working conditions, and limited opportunities for advancement? Am I not a human being first and a woman second?

Just a limited being whose opinions are automatically considered inferior, even before they're heard, who's stereotyped as "a lesser being" with no opportunity to prove the worth of her contribution on its own merits? Am I not a child of God endowed with all the dignity of being made in His image and likeness?

I am not just a woman.

I am a woman!

MAN: *(Heavy voice, guttural tones)* Me man.
You woman.
Me hunt, fish, fight.
You cook, keep kids, make clothes, and keep mouth shut.

— Ug of Ur, 4000 BC

•   •   •

MAN: *(Elizabethan Puritan tone)* Elizabeth!
It hath been said that thee hath been seen out upon the streets again today. Thou knowest a woman's place is by the hearth. If thou persisteth in this outrage of decency ano order, I must needs take away thy shoes.

— Peter Puritan

•   •   •

MAN: *(Today's husband type)* Lisa . . .
. . . did you have to show that much attention to Jim Barclay at the reception last night? It's all right to be sociable, but any conversation that's longer than a minute or two begins to look suspicious. Do you have to . . .?

WOMAN: *(Wife type)* Harry, this is today, Harry, not yesterday. You talk with others — men and women — I can talk with others — men and women. What difference does it really make? If you want to cut me off from friendships with other. . . .

MAN: *(Exasperated)* But you're a married woman now, Lisa!

WOMAN: *(Equally so)* Does that make me your sole property to be shut away from the world for your private use? That's not marriage, Harry, that's the slavery system, and I'm not going to be either slave, chattel, or second-class citizen!

36

* * *

What a change in man-woman roles!

"You've come a long way, baby, to get where you've got to today," say some who feel the major battles of the war between the sexes are won, and we are nearing a final truce. "Only the last skirmishes remain to be fought; there's a little mopping up left to be done. Then, liberty, equality, and fraternity (no!) sorority," they say.

But the war is far from history. It will not likely become history until both man and woman give up the hostility and begin to work together for peace ("peace" meaning "wholeness," at-one-ness, reconciliation, mutual trust).

Woman will not be free until man is free. Man will not be free until woman is free. Only when the old counterfeit categories — superior/inferior; stronger/weaker; intelligent/intuitive; aggressor/receptor — all come up for question, and perhaps for rejection, will we begin to experience liberation for both. The oppressor is always more bound than the oppressed, the discriminating more blind than the discriminated. And those pretending superiority are more troubled by self-doubt and insecurity than those who are stereotyped "inferior."

"To be a woman means you are an inferior being," says the aged voice of history (a male bass voice, no doubt), "therefore you must accept a subordinate, obedient position and fulfill your humble role in sweet submission."

That verdict denigrated both male and female. It colored and distorted every level of human interaction. Every expression of love and respect was tainted with the dishonesties of condescension. Love is not paternalistic; it will not reach down to the one loved. It stands alongside on a give-receive basis.

Now that superior/inferior categories are being debunked, perhaps we husbands and wives can begin to get at what maleness and femaleness actually are.

37

Now we can work at our differences as fellow humans, not as "exalted lord and master addressing most humble servant."

Now perhaps we can respect people as persons, regardless of gender, and interpersonal conflicts can be resolved in open, mutual exploration that ends in mutual satisfaction.

°　°　° this is me

HE: Honey, it says here that "the trouble with women is that they always take things personally."

SHE: Well, I don't, so there.

HE: Heh, Heh!

SHE: What's so funny?

HE: You just did. You proved the whole point.

SHE: So what's the point for debate?

HE: The difference between men and women.

SHE: You've always been for it, are you suddenly turning against it?

HE: The difference? I'm for it. As the French say, "*Vive la différence!*"

SHE: OK, let me start! The main difference in men, as I see it, is they think they're so logical, so factual, like they can prove every question that comes along with three incontrovertible truths.

HE: Come on, that's not me. . . .

SHE: Heh, heh, yourself. Now look who's taking it personal.

HE: OK . . . OK . . . so that's our problem, uh?

SHE: That — and the idea that being coldly logical is superior.

HE: Well, why not? The world was made by logic!

SHE: Huh-uh . . . the things in it, maybe, but the people were made by love.

HE: And you think women have a special claim to that?

SHE: Well, don't we? What's the difference as you see it?

HE: Oh, they're more emotional, more intuitive, more compassionate, I guess.

SHE: Love.

HE: OK, maybe they have a greater capacity to give and receive love.

SHE: Or maybe it's just that we put a higher value on it. Since loving husbands, children — and loving work — has to come first in our lives.

HE: Apparently your values keep you saner and healthier. It says here in this article I'm reading:

> In every age bracket, the death rate for men is higher than for women . . . the proportion of men in mental institutions is higher . . . there are more male alcoholics than female . . . women adjust to shock more easily than men.

SHE: Hey, hey! Whose side are you on?

HE: I'd still rather be a man.

SHE: Don't call that logic. That's pure male ego, sold on its own superiority.

HE: Huh-uh, I'm glad I'm a man so I can be your man.

SHE: There you go, making it personal again!

o   o   o

"The problem of woman's role is man's problem as well as woman's since role is fundamentally a matter of relationship," writes Lois Gunden Clemens in *Woman Liberated.* [4]

It is man's problem more than it is woman's. Man created the propaganda of inferiority. Man maintained it in social practices. Man enforced it by unjust laws and economic practices. Man decided that inferiority was decreed by Holy Scripture.

In the sixth century, the Council of Macon held serious debate over the question "Does the human female possess a soul?" They decided "yes" by a one-vote lead.

In the 1600s the Westminster Catechism, one of the

most notable expositions of Calvinism, gave instructions to wives based on 1 Peter 3:6 under the heading "the honors which inferiors owe to superiors." While 1 Peter 3:7 is for husbands under requirements "of superiors towards their inferiors."

"Deep and complex psychological conditions are involved in men's attitudes about how women are to function in society. It is more difficult for a man to identify his masculinity than for a woman to establish her femininity. Hence he has a greater problem in clarifying his role than does woman.

"A girl early becomes aware that she will grow up to be a woman like her mother. Through the maturing of her body she achieves womanhood; she realizes her femininity by becoming capable of attaining motherhood. For a boy, by contrast, growing up to be a man is not simply a natural process of bodily maturation. There are certain standards for him to meet before he will be judged as having attained manhood. He must prove himself to be a man by acquiring some trait or skill or by passing some test of achievement, . . . or an endless process of achieving in which the male must continuously prove himself to be a man." [5]

Is this an explanation for the compulsive male need, present in all societies, to pretend superiority; to plan and protect exclusive male functions, to attach position and prestige to this male prerogative? Can a man only establish his masculine identity by being superior to woman? If so, then the problem is first of all man's problem.

A great confusion exists in man-woman roles. Aggressive, competitive men, finding their identity outside themselves in skills, work, achievements, and accumulated things often refuse to recognize the worth of woman's contribution as the free individual she is. This forces some women to compete by attempting to achieve maleness, by becoming an aggressive, self-made, competitive personality. The result is often anger. Anger at the self which man had forced her to become, anger at the self she could have been in full expression of her own nature, anger at those who have confused the roles and compounded our problems of being mature men and women.

This confusion of roles, and the discrimination it produces, robs our communities of much-needed female leadership in insight, compassion, and human values. It deprives our churches of concern, committed sacrifice, of effective growth. It defrauds our families of having two complete persons interacting in freedom and integrity.

"Woman was created by her Creator, God, to be uniquely different in order to complete man. She is equal as his opposite," writes author Ella May Miller.

"Man and woman together, whether in the home or outside the home, are to represent wholeness of life. Man and woman complement." [6]

○   ○   ○

HE: Why can't you just be happy to stay home and keep house like other women?

SHE: Like which other women, your mother and grandmother? I don't want their roles.

HE: You knew when you married me that there would be a house to keep, dishes and clothes to wash, and children to care for. . . .

SHE: And you knew when you married me that there would be a yard to mow, garbage to carry out, lots of fix-it jobs, and "children to care for. . . ."

HE: Of course, but what's that got to do with it?

SHE: Everything. Marriage doesn't cut you off from a broader life and keep you home as a gardener. Why must it keep me in as a housekeeper?

HE: But that's . . . well, a wife and mother is supposed to be a wife and mother.

SHE: That's like saying a husband and father must be a husband and father. . . .

HE: OK, so you don't like being at home all the time. . . .

SHE: That's part of it. It's more that I want to be a person, with opportunities to express myself, too. Is that too much to ask?

HE: Well no, but. . . .

SHE: Who says a husband's interests are to be served first?

HE: Well, men say so, I guess.

SHE: Who says that his talents must be developed and exercised as fully as possible while the wife's potential is ignored?

HE: Well, isn't a wife supposed to find some fulfillment through her husband's achievements? Especially when she's helped him to attain his success?

SHE: Yes, of course. You know how happy I was to work while you were in college. I felt like your graduation was a milestone for us both. And having the children, that's meant everything. But next year the youngest one goes to kindergarten. So I'm free again to pick up nursing, or go back to college so I could teach . . . to get out.

HE: It really means a lot to you, doesn't it?

SHE: Does it? Put yourself in my shoes. Oh, you can't, you're a man. But just imagine how mentally impoverished you'd feel if 95 percent of your time for the last seven years had been spent in the kitchen and laundry.

HE: It's not that bad, is it?

SHE: You want to try it and let me earn the living for the next year?

HE: OK . . . OK . . . I'll quit objecting. Now, what do you want to do next fall?

SHE: I never thought you'd ask.

o   o   o

"Man's role is primary, woman's secondary. He is free to be an individual to his fullest potential, she is obligated to be an extension of his profession, or one of his possessions."

Stated boldly, that is the false premise on which many marriages stand. The man tends to view his wife as one of the many important pieces of property, along with his house, his automobile, his boat, his office. She helps establish and confirm both his self-image and his public image. Such a wife soon comes to understand that she is something less than a full person in her husband's thinking.

If she finds him relating to her largely on a physical level, as a sexual partner, she comes to feel deep resentment at being only a sex symbol and object. A husband whose major values are bustline, hipline, hemline may temporarily stimulate his wife to concentrate on making herself the most attractive sexual commodity in the local market, but eventually it degrades love instead of fulfilling it.

If she finds him relating to her mainly as master-servant, employer-employee, or executive-assistant, she comes to feel exploited, as she actually is. And this destroys true acceptance and respect for both. Decisions must be mutual. Those who claim the right to command others without sharing the responsibility of deciding, communicate self-conceit, insensitivity, and pride of power even though their words protest it.

Male and female were created in the image of God. Equally. Two parts of one unity, man. Man-he and man-she, as the Hebrew of Genesis 1:26, 27 expressed it.

God's view of man and woman sees them as two parts of human personhood, each needing to be completed by the other. Each is incomplete when alone. One part of Man cannot be considered superior to another. Both must make their complementary contribution. Not in competition, but in cooperation to complete each other's inadequate perspective on life. Not in duplication, but with difference of viewpoint each supplies to the other what that other lacks.

"Man and woman, venturing forth side by side in mutual trust will learn through . . . experience how God has destined them to function together. The fact that mankind was created as a sexual duality indicates that man and woman as separate persons have been given no completely fixed or clearly defined roles. Rather they have been called to be partners in all of life. But to live creatively in this partnership, they must be ready to renounce what is simply traditional, as opposed to what is really biblical, in their views of each other." [7]

Two persons. Two personalities. One unity. The two-ness must not be engulfed by the one-ness. Each remains distinct with an integrity of his/her own. Both for each retain the privilege of reaching out for their full potential, to discover their own completeness as whole persons.

A woman must be first, her own person; second, her husband's wife; and then, her child's mother. Finding fulfillment in equality, integrity, and unity.

o o o

"I, John,
    Take thee, Mary,
        To be my lawfully wedded wife.
            I will love and cherish thee. . . ."

"I, Mary,
    Take thee, John,
        To be my lawfully wedded husband.
            I will love, honor, and obey. . . ."

Obey? Why not love and respect? Or love and share? The Bible says "obey" many Christians (male) have sternly said. Only a century ago, in 1857, F. A. Ross, a Presbyterian minister in Dixie used the subjection of wives as an assured base to approve slavery and to prove it "ordained of God."

> Do you say the slave is held in involuntary servitude? So is the wife! [The husband] has authority from God to rule over you. You are bound to obey him in all things. You cannot leave your parlor, nor your bedchamber, nor your couch, if your husband commands you to stay there." [8]

What does the Bible ask? Genesis 1:26-28 and 2:23, 24 record the first significant words on man-woman relationships, and no distinction is made between husband and wife except that man is shown taking the initiative. After the fall — Genesis 3 — a difference begins to appear. But this is man-woman relating in their fallen state, tainted by evil, hostile in accusation, competitive in their self-interests. In sin, man demands mastery, exacts obedience, and attempts to dominate.

Christ showed no favoritism. He offered no superior respect to either man or woman. He accepted each as equals, gave each the same dignity and worth, related to male and female with identical trust and compassion.

In Christ the fall is revoked. We are freed. The distinctions between male and female are erased because "you are all one in Christ Jesus" (Gal. 3:28 and its parallel, Col. 3:11).

But what of Peter's word to wives commanding submissiveness and reverent obedience? 1 Peter 3:1-12.

His word to wives was written to women married within a Roman system which considered them as little more than slaves. With the Romans, a woman remained forever a child. As the father had life or death power over her, so later did the husband. Infidelity or drunkenness were punishable by death. Divorce came on any pretext.

In Greek civilization a woman was to stay indoors, see as little, hear as little, ask as little, know as little as necessary.

45

She had no independent existence, no will or mind of her own. Divorce was at the man's caprice.

Under Jewish law, the husband owned the wife as he owned sheep or goats. Under no circumstances could she leave him. He could dismiss her on a whim.

In all ancient civilizations a woman did not dare take any decision upon herself. To convert to another religion was unthinkable.

So Peter's advice to practice simple, submissive, reverent Christian witness was absolutely necessary. But it did not indicate the norm for Christian couples. Verses 7-12 indicate their new position of equality, as fellow heirs of the grace of life.

In the New Testament, husband-wife relationships first are elevated to partnership. Men/women functioned in co-ministries as did Aquila and Priscilla. The apostles traveled with their wives in mission journeys, a strangely revolutionary action for those times. 1 Cor. 9:5, TEV.

Paul introduced the most complete statement in the New Testament on marriage with a command for both to be submissive to each other. Ephesians 5:21. He even saw fit to simply repeat that instruction for the woman, laying no heavier burden on her.

But to the man he gave the great command — love sacrificially with the same quality of self-giving which Christ showed to us. That is what it means for man to be "head." Christ's headship was achieved through service to leadership. Through self-sacrifice to discovery.

 And that is to be the character of a man's leadership. Submissive self-giving. He leads out, Christlike, in self-giving as did his Lord. And the wife responds by being "subject to [her] husband as is fitting in the Lord" (Col. 3:18, RSV.) Man's headship is the responsibility for taking the initiative. It is not authority and domination. He, too, must learn to submit.

The man has the responsibility of initiating and coordinating the cooperative effort which supports their life together. As partners they respect and reverence each other as equals, although different in kind. Their differences of masculinity and femininity give neither superiority nor inferiority to either one of the two; rather, these differences are complementary as each partner brings some special area of superiority to contribute to the other. Both are free to contribute to the partnership the best of their own personhood. [9]

"But for the wife, submission also means subordination, doesn't it?"

Submission is subordination? Yes, then both are subordinate to the self-giving life-style of the One who chose to be a servant. Yes, when the man accepts the woman's subordination as a challenge to submit himself to her in mutual service. Yes, when both take the servant style as the pattern for their lives together.

47

CHAPTER FOUR

To Communicate Demands . . .

"I love you."

Three little words. Simple words. Transparent. Completely unmistakable. "I love you."

Say them aloud, Softly. Gently. How could anyone fail to understand their meaning? "I love you."

Unless they are said in a different way. What if the inflection were changed to "I love you?" or "I? Love you?" If it is tinged with sarcasm — "I *love* you!" — the meaning can totally reverse itself, leap from intimacy to insult.

After a decade of communications research, Albert Mehrabian has attempted to unravel the tangled secrets of our conversations with each other. He suggests the following formula to express the accurate proportions between the content of our words and the way they are expressed: words alone, 7 percent; tone of voice and inflection, 38 percent. The remaining 55 percent? It is found in facial expressions, our posture, and in the gestures we use. [10]

"I love you."

The same three words can be said with many meanings — as many as there are possible inflections. And that number can be squared by the number of potential meanings each of those inflections would have to each of the three billion people in our world.

Communication is the meeting of meaning.

When your meaning meets my meaning across the bridge of words, tones, acts, and deeds, when understanding occurs, then we know we have communicated.

When three little words — I love you — are spoken, heard, felt, and believed, it's not just a matter of communicating what you thought. We are communicating what we are by what we are.

o   o   o

In marriage, we do not choose — on occasion — to communicate. We are constantly in communication with each other whether negatively or positively. In fact, we cannot NOT communicate. We are our communication.

o   o   o

When two people say they have a problem in communication, they have a problem to be sure. But it's not in communication. Lack of acceptance, perhaps. Or fear of intimacy. Or anxiety about opening their lives to each other. But not likely communication.

o   o   o

It is not the ability to communicate that is lost when marriages grow apart. It is the desire to communicate that undergoes change. When one or the other no longer wants to be understood or to be understanding, then distance will develop.

o   o   o

Love is the opening of one's life to another in intimate, understanding communication. When two persons can share from the very center of their existence, they experience love in its truest quality. Marriage is a venture into intimacy, and intimacy is the opening of one self to another.

o   o   o

SHE: I love being close to you. . . .
HE: Uh-huh. . . .
SHE: Why can't we always feel just like this?
HE: Like this?
SHE: Mmm! Close. Together. And open.
HE: Don't crowd me, June.
SHE: Don't crowd you, Ron? What kind of answer is that?
HE: Just don't crowd me, that's all I ask.
SHE: (Aside) Been married seven years and he says I shouldn't crowd him.
HE: Good night.
SHE: Good night! Oh, no you don't. You're not withdrawing into a dream world just like that!
HE: Who's withdrawing? I just want some sleep.
SHE: Sleep! You want to avoid me.
HE: I just don't want you or anybody breathing down my neck.
SHE: You want to isolate yourself from me.
HE: I do not, I am not . . . well . . . I guess we've just got different ideas of marriage. For you, it's living in mental, well, in emotional nudity. And I can't stand being that close to anybody, at least not for long. Occasionally, maybe, but if you think marriage gives you license to go exploring inside my head any time you want, then I'm gonna run!
SHE: You're going to run?
HE. Yes, run! I can't stay that close to anyone . . . even you . . . without smothering. I need room to breathe,

elbowroom, or I get uptight.

SHE: You get panicky because you're afraid of intimacy. You won't open up except when you have to, like to get close for sex or something.

HE: Don't bring that in. We get along fine on that score, but why can't you leave well enough alone?

SHE: Maybe because it isn't well enough for me. Maybe because I'd like to feel close to you in other ways, too. But you won't open up to me like I do to you. Maybe because I think marriage should mean more to us than it does.

HE: All right . . . all right, now you've got us pegged, so can I get some sleep?

SHE: So you push me away. Sure, go to sleep if that's the most important thing to you.

HE: Humh. . . .

SHE: Good night?

HE: Sure . . . good night!

o o o

Partners vary greatly in their need for privacy or their readiness for intimacy. Some persons are compulsively eager to share everything with their partners and then demand that they reciprocate. But such a decision must be mutual. Others fear transparency and seek to protect their privacy at all costs.

The desire for an intimate understanding for each other's emotional capacities is the base of good communications in marriage. But such intimate communication is not a note tendered in marriage and thereafter payable upon demand.

Intimacy of mind is a gift. Freely given. It is offered, not upon request, but in response to another's willingness to open his or her self in sharing. As we sense acceptance, understanding, and forgiveness extended to us by another, we are freed to give love and trust.

Such a relationship cannot be forced. Nothing stymies communication like the persistent prying of a partner who insists on "breaking and entering" another's privacy; although general understanding may often result best from conflict which cleans up old "grudge" items and clears the air for a more honest love-relationship.

Openness with each other is a skill which must be learned. It is not a talent possessed by some at birth, like a musical ear. It's an ability to be acquired in maturing. Maturing in communication, maturing in handling conflict, maturing in giving and receiving love.

A growing love-relationship of intimacy is not easily achieved.

To those romantic idealists who envision it as a saccharine-sweet harmony that is never marred by conflict, never tensed up by frustrations we must say, "the exact reverse." Where two people continue in flawless coexistence, doing their silent pantomime of perfection, with their "ideal mate," genuine intimacy is impossible. Its first gentle nudge would puncture their dream world and explode their gossamer "harmony."

In intimate relationships "ignorance is not bliss." It leads to unbearable boredom and conceals unbelievable anger. To be intimate is "to know."

To those practical realists who spurn honest conversation and candid exposure of their true feelings and choose instead the way of withdrawal we must say, "No openness and intimacy." Intimacy is not available to the loner, the shrinking violets who play-it-safe-we-might-uncover-a-conflict. Or the "people-don't-change" crowd who say, "What's the use? We know where we stand, so what?"

In intimate relationships, familiarity does not breed contempt, but respect. True familiarity that brings two to deeper understanding is a fundamental for growing love.

o   o   o

SHE: Sometimes I get to feeling, "Sure, we've been married for nine years, but we still don't know each other."

HE: Must be because we were never properly introduced.

SHE: There you go again, joking to turn off an uncomfortable subject.

HE: It's more like an unanswerable riddle.

SHE: That's what our marriage is to you? That's what it is?

HE: No . . . no, the riddle is why you want to keep taking it apart and looking at what makes it tick.

SHE: But it doesn't tick much. And when it does, it sounds more like a time bomb.

HE: So what's going to explode?

SHE: Not what . . . who.

HE: Then who?

SHE: How should I know? Maybe me, maybe you. Do you realize this is the most we've talked in five years?

HE: Helen, I've told you a million times not to exaggerate.

SHE: There you go with another one-liner. Do you have to joke at a time like this?

HE: Better joke than blow up.

SHE: A blow-up would be better than a stalemate. No, don't pun on that one. I can't take it.

HE: You're really serious about this, aren't you?

SHE: Serious? I'm desperate. If we can't get something better going for us — like opening up and understanding each other — I've had it. I've got to know how you really feel about things.

HE: When I tell you how I feel, you clam up.

SHE: You tell me in a one-liner and I'm supposed to figure out what it means. And if I take you seriously you tell me it was just a joke.

HE: Well, you'd make a federal case out of it otherwise.

SHE: That's just because I have to pick a fight to get you to talk!

HE: I talk. You just don't listen.

SHE: You hint. You don't talk it out.

HE: Well, what do you call all this?

SHE: I'd call it just talking about talking. When do we get to the real thing?

HE: Like what?

SHE: Oh, like when do you quit renting and go looking for a house to buy?

HE: So that's what was behind all this?

SHE: No . . . there you go again, blaming it on something. Can't you see the problem is us?

HE: My problem is it's 10:30. I'm turning in. If you'd like the last word, help yourself. Your next line is it.

o   o   o

Afraid of conflict.

Afraid of intimacy.

Afraid of understanding.

Afraid to communicate.

Afraid to love.

Safety in silent retreat is cloaked in smiles.

Escape into quiet withdrawal is covered with humor.

Intimacy is evaded by denying that distance exists — (Problem? What problem?); insisting that all is well — (It suits me fine.); bristling when the status quo is threatened — (Don't start looking under rocks again.); or avoiding all responsibility — (There's nothing wrong. It's all in your head.).

What alternatives are open to a couple when communications seem clogged?

Candid conversation seems impossible. Of course, that is the end to be reached, not necessarily the means to be used.

Creative conflict may be able to blow out the pipes and clear out old obstructions. However, our hostilities may conceal all kinds of quirks in our personal makeups that contort our handling of anger into weirdly abusive and destructive schemes that mask themselves with childlike innocence. (This will be explored in the next chapter.)

Appreciative empathy may open the way. Letting go of the other person emotionally and seeking simply to appreciate and understand may begin to unfog cloudy conversation and unchoke channels of communication stopped up with all kinds of emotional blocks.

As long as one marriage partner is seeking to control or dominate by one hold or other, communication is cramped by the emotional arm-twist that is applied at any moment of tension. And that attempted domination may be so subtle — an air of disapproval. An attitude of superiority. A reoccurring judgmental look. A penchant for criticizing. It's a general refusal to appreciate, to empathize, and to love.

Appreciative empathy begins in *hearing*, hearing deeply. In picking up, beyond words spoken, the feeling, the implied but unexpressed meanings, the inaudible signals of the other personality. Empathy seeks to catch a whisper of the deep human cry that is within us all, perhaps buried and unknown. Or to hear just the edge of the silent scream of loneliness and pain that another carries.

Can you hear the sounds and meanings of another's life and resonate to them? Can you try to listen to someone at all the levels present in their self-communication?

In marriage, where years of life together should make such many-leveled communication easier (so silence could be truly golden), too often the reverse is true. Years of unresolved conflicts and frustration accumulate like emotional baggage. Our past experience becomes not an open door to deeper understanding, but a screened window which filters out everything unacceptable and lets us receive only what we want to hear.

Can you hear without prejudging the other, without presuming to know what he or she is going to say before it is said, and hearing only what you expect to hear? Can you listen without the misunderstanding that springs from your own frustrations?

It feels good to hear, to truly hear, and to see in the other's eyes that they know they've been heard. There's a gentleness in the eyes, a moistness touched with gratitude when a person realizes, "I've been heard for what I am. Someone else now knows what it is to be me."

o   o   o

A parable: Two miles down, four miles out in the black tunnels of a coal mine, there is a sudden explosion. Gas ignites. The ceiling falls. Men are buried alive. Only one survives, trapped in a distant, forgotten tunnel. One day, digging despairingly at the rockfall, he finds an electrical conduit protruding from the rubble-blocked passageway. Hope awakens. Perhaps it might carry a sound through the rock mass to the rescue crew, if they have not abandoned the search. He seizes a rock, and taps out his SOS in Morse code. Days pass. Still he taps, then pauses to listen for an answering signal. "What's the use?" he wonders. "I'm forgotten. No one knows I'm alive. No one cares. What's the point of trying? Why not quit and die?"

Then, one day, a whisper of a tap comes back down the pipe. He taps again to be sure. The answering sound is more definite. He sits, transfused with liquid joy, even though his dehydrated body cannot squeeze his tears of relief through his dust-clotted tear ducts. "Someone knows I'm here," he says over and over. "I've been heard."

It feels so good to be heard. To be heard without the listener judging, trying to mold you, even trying to help by changing you. It feels good just to be heard with a touch of appreciation. To know that somebody else knows what it feels like to be trapped inside the undesirable/desirable body and personality of yours and they didn't turn away in shock and disgust. They stood with you in your pain.

Communication happens when a man or woman has been truly heard and willingly understood. Problems may still remain, but in the moment the load is shared by someone else it is possible for the bearer to get a fresh look at his situation. And the insolvable, insolvable though it is, may begin slowly to dissolve.

When two people can truly hear each other, knowing there's nothing to be afraid of, they experience a release, a sense of freedom. No longer do they need to keep their guard up, no need to go on wearing armor. Communication is doing its liberating work, the work which creates true emotional-mental intimacy. It is at its best when each experiences it, and each knows that the other is experiencing it. Such intimate sharing may not happen frequently, but unless it does happen on occasion, we are not fully human. Not authentically human. [11]

Have you noticed in the Gospels that it happened with startling frequency for Jesus? Whenever, in fact, He met another human who was willing to drop his mask of pride or pretense and come out from behind his armor. No such fortune with the Pharisees who entered into conversation only from a position of impregnable superiority.

The Jesus-way was to come on with no pretenses, to open Himself to others and initiate a person-to-person relationship. He was willing to lend a hand where He could help them off with their armor (i.e., the gentle prying at a rusty hinge on Nicodemus' helmet visor — John 3:10-12); the tactful way He informed the Samaritan woman that her see-through armor wasn't covering too well — John 4:17-19; or even the candid offer to the affluent young nobleman to trade in his silver-plated suit for a new cut of clothes — Mark 10:17-22. But he left their privacy intact if they hung out the "Do Not Disturb" sign.

Except when He chose to use conflict. And no one ever exercised it more creatively. His purpose in confronting others was invariably redemptive. He would hold up a verbal mirror that reflected what and where they truly were (e.g., Matthew 23:13-39).

The Jesus-way began with listening. He could hear. He proceeded with gentle understanding. He could feel with another. He assisted without violating another's freedom. He could respect. Occasionally, He awakened the other with a jolt of reality. He could love enough to be honest. He always reached out in appreciation and forgiveness. He could accept.

That is what it means to be fully human. That is person-to-person communication fully achieved.

o   o   o

What happens when marriage partners become hard of hearing? (Something has to be said twice and underlined in red as it's said.) Or selective listeners? (Each hears what he/she wants to hear; all else is filtered out.) Or tone deaf? (The feeling-tones and innuendos go by unnoticed.)

Anger is what happens. Each becomes angry when the other obviously will not hear. And the speaker feels like saying, "Oh, what's the use, anyway? I can't get through, he's turned off." Such anger makes a person feel terribly alone.

Rejection follows. With a long period of treatment punctuated by intermittent hostilities. As one wife records in a verbatim transcript of her husband's total conversation from the minute he entered the door in the evening until he went to bed:

6:10 "Any mail?"

6:25 "Tell the kids to get that darned dog to stop barking."

6:35 "Don't you know how to fix anything but meat loaf?"

6:50 "Pass the sugar."
7:10 "How come the newspaper is wet?"
7:45 "Change the channel. This is lousy."
10:30 "Walk the hound. I'm going to bed."

o   o   o

Suspicion breeds in noncommunicative relationships. Each becomes expert at camouflaging his/her real meaning. (Wondering, "Will he/she get the hint?") And both find they must explore the many possibilities of each line of conversation and narrow down the meanings to a few possibles.

HE: Jim Blakes had another baby yesterday.
SHE: Really?
HE: Yes, finally they've got a boy. On their third try.
SHE: Their third accident, likely.

This not-so-simple conversational gambit may contain an amazing variety of messages.

Hers may be: 1. Nobody chooses to have more than two kids, beyond that it's a miss-conception. 2. Stop bugging me that we only have one girl. It's the male that determines sex, you know. 3. Why didn't they adopt and save us one less population surplus? 4. I know I'm nearing menopause, don't rub it in. 5. So you once dated Catherine Blake. You think she might have enjoyed sex more and not have been so worried about pregnancy.

His meanings could be: 1. You complain about caring for one child on our budget; they've got three, have less income, and still have a new car. 2. Remember when we had a little one around the house? Imagine them doing it again, and at 38. 3. You could give me a son, if you'd just let me flush those pills down the toilet. 4. Why were you so panicky last time your period was late? It wouldn't be so bad. 5. What kind of woman are you? Acting the martyr bit after one childbirth, and handing me the same line each time we start to make love?

o   o   o

Why are communications such a tangled problem in marriage? Why is it that husbands and wives must not speak so they can be understood but also speak so they cannot be misunderstood?

It may be because of faulty assumptions. "He knows how I feel about that. I've told him often enough. If he does not know it, it's all his fault."

It may be unrealistic expectations. "If you really love me, you'll understand what I want. Love is never even needing to say it. If you really click together, you just know what the other wants, somehow."

It may even be requiring impossible conditions. "Unless he notices my new blouse, I'm not speaking. If he doesn't express appreciation for my cleaning up his desk I won't talk to him all evening.

o   o   o

"Communication can be called the core of any successful marriage. When you fail to listen to each other and to talk to each other, there is deep trouble ahead. . . . Love can survive large problems in the open better than small ones buried and smoldering within. . . . Thinking together is more important than thinking alike. And talking together about touchy problems indicates true love for each other. Communication puts love into practice." [12]

o   o   o

"Intimate communication involves a lot more than transmitting and receiving signals. Its purpose is to make explicit everything that partners expect of each other — what is most agreeable and least agreeable, what is relevant and irrelevant; to monitor continually what they experience as bonding or alienating; to synchronize interests, habits, and "hang-ups"; and to effect the fusion that achieves the *we* without demolishing the *you* or the *me*." [13]

。　。　。

Communication never ends. What we are to one another cannot be silenced. What we say to each other by our words should resonate with our deeds, acts, and gifts to the other. Successful marriages are built by partners who achieve consistent communications both verbally and non-verbally. There will always be discrepancies. But they can be reduced to understandable minimums and overlooked in love if couples work at consistent communication and constant love.

CHAPTER FIVE

To Make Conflict Creative . . .

"Eye for an Aye or Tooth for a Truth"
A drama in numberless acts (of violence)

CAST *(Dramatis Personae)*

1. Nellie Nagger: Noted for shrewd, critical insight; takes pride in her powers of memory, never forgets a fault in others. Can recall date, time of day, and exact details for every act or word said or done against her. What she can recall, she does! Favorite words: "You always do this. . . ." or, "You never do that."
2. Burt Battler: Presents a surface impression of easygoing masculinity, but is highly skilled in friction-making. Often irritable due to deep resources of undersurface hostility. Strikes back instantly when he suspects attack. The complete hawk. Favorite line: "Sometimes you burn me up."

3. Gert Gunnysacker: Constantly collecting grievances. Broods over complaints until she reaches the bursting point. Refuses to deal with individual problems as they arise. Reserves them until they've grown out of all proportions, then threatens to detonate. Final explosion is usually touched off by some trifle. Favorite tactic: silence. Favorite line when collecting: "I don't want to talk about it." Favorite line when exploding: "I've had it up to here."

4. Orville Overkill: When conflict threatens he quickly attacks with the most terrible line available to him, dropping an A-bomb on an anthill. His instincts are to annihilate all opposition. Or he may be at times even-tempered and able to absorb a lot of flak, but when provoked beyond his limits he will "go for the jugular" by striking at any painful sore spot his wife wants forgotten. Favorite line: "At least I never did what you. . . ."

5. Willie Withdrawn: A genuine dove. Would rather flee than fight. Lapses into long silences in any situation of threat. If hostility continues, takes long walks or goes for a drive. Most spoken lines: "I can't take any more. I'm getting out of here."

6. Vivian Vesuvius: Even-tempered and good-natured except when in eruption. No signals to warn of approaching volcanic activity. When Vesuvius lets go, a great blast of scalding steam blows off her accumulated overload of free-floating, undirected hostility. Favorite words: Anything available in the heat of anger.

7. Annie Analyst: A constant mate-watcher who is ever analyzing his character, interpreting his motives, relating them to his childhood (or childishness), stereotyping him by the actions that peeve her most. Fond of labeling her mate in pseudopsychological jargon. "I know your type. You're a. . . ."

o   o   o

ACT XLVII
Scene 1

SETTING: *Kitchen of a suburban split-level, Middle-class decor. Wife at stove, stewing emotionally, warming over last night's feud, and stirring up this evening's big beef!*

(Enter husband at front door)

BURT BATTLER-TYPE: Hi, dear, I'm home.

GERT GUNNYSACKER-TYPE: And only *one* hour late. You must have been speeding. Or wasn't there any traffic?

BURT: The usual.

GERT: How were things at the office?

BURT: Awful. As usual. Do you have to be forever asking? (Lifts lids on pots at stove)
Stew again. I see my being late couldn't have damaged any culinary triumphs you'd planned.

GERT: You don't miss a day, do you? (First signs of impending explosion)

BURT: What?

GERT: You gripe about my cooking every day of the year and twice on Sunday.

BURT: Cut it out, Gert. I make an occasional suggestion, maybe, but I give you your share of compliments too.

GERT: Yesterday you complimented the liver, right? Was it "fried tongue of shoe" you named it? The day before you called the dessert something I wouldn't repeat.

BURT: (Moves to put his arm around her) Aw, c'mon, Gert!

GERT: Don't touch me, you . . . you . . . the first thing you walk in the door, you start criticizing, you. . . .

BURT: (Starting to yell) I did no such thing. (Slams table) What's the use? Any more of this and I'm gonna let you have one you won't forget.

•   •   •

64

Scenes 2 through 5 take place in the respective kitchens of other couples in the cast. We spare your needing to read them because nothing is more tedious and monotonous than other people's marital battles. But let him/her that is without sin stone the cast first, or first cast the stone.

o   o   o

"And so they lived happily ever after."

(Two lovers walk hand in hand into the sunset. Fade-out)

That's how it should end. Always. With no exceptions. Every romantic knows that.

But it never does. True, people can and do achieve happiness together. But not through simple hand-holding in a scene softened by the rose tones of the setting sun.

Marital happiness is won through conflict. Even through conflicts about conflict. But only through conflict that is turned creative through understanding. Creative conflict can be the force that impels us to break through to true emotional intimacy.

What is this condition, "conflict"?

It is emotional tensions caused by the clash of two or more persons' needs/drives/goals/values, and their individual ways of expressing or fulfilling of these needs/drives/goals/values. Such a clash may be used constructively to help partners clear the air of misunderstanding and straighten out their goals. Conflict is the most common atmosphere in which change — creative change — takes place.

Erich Fromm, the noted psychoanalyst, somewhere writes: "The man who cannot create, wants to destroy." These are the two options that lie open before us in our conflicts — to create or to destroy. When two contrasting or competing personalities seek to relate on a continuing basis as in marriage, conflict is inevitable. Used creatively, this conflict can become a source of rich experiences in growing understanding. Conflicts can become a means of negotiating wholesome and satisfactory adjustments.

But like any high explosive, it must be handled with skill and care lest the sparks struck by our friction touch off violent anger and resentment!

o   o   o

If we are to work with conflicts safely and even creatively, we will need to defuse a few of the fears and mistaken ideas we hold hidden in the secret storehouse of our hostilities. Unless we do, they can easily trigger a serious conflagration.

o   o   o

?	?
Anger is the opposite of love. If you are angry, you do not love.	Apathy is the opposite of love. Anger indicates that the other person's attitudes and actions matter much.
Conflict kills love. If you have conflicts, your marriage is in mortal danger.	Love does not mean an absence of conflict, nor does conflict indicate an absence of love. Conflict is love testing the strength of its ties to the other.
Conflicts are little things that keep cropping up and spoiling everything. Little things alone can do a marriage in.	Most of what we call "conflicts" tend to be symptoms; minor, superficial disagreements which are often a cover for the real conflicts beneath the surface. Both are important, but the crucial ones are usually the differences that remain hidden.
Each individual difference must be taken seriously and dealt with thoroughly as it comes up or it will always be there to bug you.	Many minor differences should be accepted with humor and treated with a smile. If we get hung up on these little frictions that clutter our daily relationships, we may never get down to dealing with the real differences.

| A husband or wife can always tell you what's really bugging them if you just listen and take what they tell you literally. | Most husband-wife conflicts tend to come out indirectly over substitute issues and often stalemate unless careful listening brings the central differences into the open. |

"One can easily get in over his/her head by opening deeper conflicts," many couples conclude. "Better let sleeping dogs lie." Actual differences can and eventually must be examined in honest self-disclosure. With the help of a counselor, they can be used constructively to open new areas of understanding and closeness. Often the conflicts have done such damage to the feelings of one or both that it is unrealistic to attempt working it out without help. Do not wait too long before summoning a third party. Too many "do-it-yourself" patch jobs tear away more than they correct. Help is worth whatever it costs your pride.

○ ○ ○

SHE: What do you mean, "I'm hostile to you"? That's not fair.

HE: Not fair? You call "foul" when I just state the truth about our relationship?

SHE: I'm not hostile, that's why. I've never lost my temper and said things I need to be sorry about.

HE: No, you haven't. If there's any threat of hostility, you clam up.

SHE: That way I've got nothing to be sorry about.

HE: Don't say that again. It sounds so self-righteous, so all-sufferingly noble of you.

SHE: It's the truth.

HE: Oh, no it's not. It's not even a half-truth. You use silence like a weapon. Your silence is violence.

SHE: "Silence is golden," I've always said.

HE: That line's been worth its weight in gold to you, hasn't it? You've used it to buy your way out of many uncomfortable conversations.

SHE: I don't want to talk about it anymore.

HE: That's not surprising. It's getting a little close, isn't it?

SHE: That's not it. I just don't like this kind of talk. I've always been big enough to overlook our differences. What's wrong with that?

HE: I'll tell you what's wrong with it. Whatever husbands and wives refuse to talk out, they act out.

SHE: You mean. . . .?

HE: I mean your anger at me comes out in many ways. You pride yourself at never losing your cool. So you repress it all and take it out on me day after day.

SHE: I do nothing of the sort.

HE: Don't you? You know how you scald me with silence anytime I step across your imaginary lines.

SHE: I said, I don't want to talk about it anymore.

HE: Here we go again, same old routine.

o   o   o

Some people will stop at nothing to avoid dealing with conflict. There's the "give in-quickly-before-someone-is-hurt" dodge. Or the "if-we-don't-talk-about-it-won't-it-go-away?" maneuver. Or the "sure-we-could-talk-it-out-but-there's-no-suitable-time-or-place" excuse.

Such caution is not only pure cowardice, it is potentially disastrous.

Anger and conflict can only be constructive when handled realistically without dishonest hidden strategies. When it is denied or repressed, it creates coldness, distance, and rigidity in all relationships.

Erik Erikson, one of the leading theorists on emotional maturity blames the failure to achieve human intimacy in marriage on "the inability to engage in controversy and useful combat." [14]

Dr. George Bach, in his fascinating book *The Intimate*

Enemy (a handbook on how to fight fair in love and marriage), says: "We believe, then, that there can be no mature intimate relationship without aggressive leveling; that is, "having it out," speaking up, asking the partner "what's eating him," and negotiating for realistic settlements of differences. This does cause stress, but . . . the pain of conflict is the price of true and enduring love. People simply cannot release all their love feelings unless they have learned to manage their hate." [15]

Conflict, resolved creatively, results in greater intimacy, understanding and acceptance. Is that not sufficient reason for welcoming it, if not eagerly, at least without fear?

Fear one: overcoming fear of conflict itself. It's difficult to admit how afraid we actually are of being open enough to fight with each other. Some of our most elaborate defense systems are designed to conceal this fear.

A wife may weave a continuous network of good reasons for avoiding it. "Not in the house, the children will hear; not in the car, we'll have an accident; not in the bedroom, it will turn us off physically; not in front of friends, it will cause gossip; not when we're walking in the park, the dog gets nervous and barks."

A husband will develop his own repertoire of evasions. "I've got to work late, don't wait for me at supper; forget breakfast, I've got an early appointment; I've got no choice, the boss made this golf date for me, I'll be gone all day Saturday; don't wake me, I deserve to sleep in Sunday morning; not now, Dear, I'm reading the paper. Sorry, this is the game of the season, I can't miss it."

The roots of this fear may go back to a childhood revulsion to the unfair fights the parents fought. Or the techniques of withdrawal may have been lifted intact from the parents' handling of conflict. The pattern may have been further nourished by a mistaken piety or religious practice of repressing hostilities in a vain attempt at pretending perfection. Or there are those who feel an obligation to profess a great freedom from all human angers when such release is neither promised nor provided by religious faith. (Faith teaches us to confess anger honestly and deal with it promptly. Faith affirms that anger, controlled by love, can convert quick flashes of temper to a warm flow of compassion and concern.)

Fear of expressed anger must be rejected. The fear can be replaced by faith. A faith that anger need not wedge you apart. A faith that no difference or difficulty need force a great distance between you which forgiveness cannot surmount.

Dr. William Menninger, noted psychiatrist and marriage counselor, has some very crucial insights on expressing anger: "Do not talk when angry," he says, "but after you have calmed down, do talk. Sometimes we push each other away and the problem between us festers and festers. Just as in surgery, free and adequate drainage is essential if healing is to take place." [16]

Fear two: fear of follow-through. Don't be afraid to follow through on a fight. It's not too difficult to get a conflict open. Anger usually takes care of that for us. And it's not too difficult to name the issues at stake as each sees them. But it is hard to stay with it until it is all the way to resolution.

No solution can arise until people are willing to examine what is making them angry and explore it in two-way discussion. (Discussion, not argument.) The line between discussing and arguing is a fine distinction at times. Where it is drawn may depend on which one draws it first. Perhaps the really helpful distinction is that in discussion either party should be able at any time to summarize and play back the other person's point of view in a way that is satisfactory to that person. In argument, each is generally preparing a rebuttal while the opposition is stating its case.

The purpose of such discussion must be clearly defined: new understanding, new reconciliation. Otherwise, it simply salts the open wounds. Talking it out is only one part of the follow-through. Few couples are evenly matched in verbal skills and logical wits. All discussion and no pause for introspection and consideration of the other's viewpoint makes reconciliation a spoil to be carried off every time by the extrovert.

A couple must learn the rhythm of discussion followed by meditation; then questioning followed with consideration; then challenge leading to other's-point-of-view-seeing; until conversation results in understanding.

Only a partial solution will be found when no-trespassing signs mark off areas which dare not be explored. Many couples keep these no-man's-land border zones on various fronts of their relationship. Often they mark permanent ceasefire lines where an old hostility has stalemated and lies unsatisfactorily resolved to both, but too dangerous to re-inspect. Unresolved anger is like a fire that gets into the framework of a house. It can and will break out again at unexpected and unexplainable points.

Of course, neither husband nor wife has the right to force his or her way into the other's "keep out" areas. Honest openness is won, not demanded. Each is responsible to open his own hurts and resentments for healing and to reach out with understanding as an invitation for the other to recip-rocate. To rush in by force is to crush the other's freedom and intensify the anger.

As such "keep out" zones accumulate and slowly cut off advance or retreat on more fronts, a couple moves slowly into "emotional divorce" where each has cut the other off internally even though convenience or obligation keeps them deadlocked in wedlock.

"Morbidity marriage" it may be better termed. It is nearness without closeness; familiarity without intimacy; cohabitation without cooperation or communication. Life in common with no love and communion.

Conflict, once initiated, must be completed. Follow through! This is the point of St. Paul's words to the Christians at Ephesus.

> If you are angry, be sure that it is not out of wounded pride or bad temper. Never go to bed angry — don't give the devil that sort of foothold.
>
> Let there be no more resentment, no more anger or temper, no more violent self-assertiveness, no more slander and no more malicious remarks. Be kind to one another; be understanding. Be as ready to forgive others as God for Christ's sake has forgiven you (Eph. 4:26, 27, 31, 32).

Note the wisdom of Paul's counsel on resolving anger. "Keep short accounts," he says, "settle each day's anger debits by the end of that day. Don't give the devil the foothold he desires by letting anger sour overnight and slowly ferment into resentment and long-term hostility. End the day, or better yet each experience of conflict, with kindness and forgiveness."

Fear three: fear of losing the fight. When a husband or wife fights to win, with the declared objective of forcing the other to admit defeat, then everyone loses.

When husband and wife enter conflict, each afraid of losing, each determined to win alone, they seldom realize they are attempting the impossible.

Marital conflict is not a win/lose matter. It is a win/win or a lose/lose kind of fight. Defeat or victory are never experienced by only one of a pair. Both win — in creative resolution of the conflict — or both lose in widening gaps in understanding. But when one sets out to win alone, he or she is tempted to use foul tactics that only lovers have access to and anger enough to utilize.

The husband or wife who is out to win by inflicting a loss on the other can hardly fight fair. To down the other and come out alone on top of the heap you've got to hit below the belt. "All's fair in love and war," the old proverb says. "All's fair in love and at war," some husbands and wives conclude.

Fear — fear of losing what cannot be won — forces mates to fight foul.

°   °   °

SHE: A new shirt and tie. She must be some secretary to deserve all that.

HE: There's no secretary involved in this mess. But if there were, she wouldn't have to be much to compete with you right now.

SHE: So why'd you marry me, anyway?

HE: Not for the seven a.m. spectacular in kimono and curlers that shuffles around this kitchen, that's for sure.

SHE: Huh!

HE: Have you considered serving breakfast again sometime? (She ignores him) Oh, forget it. There's no time left. (He gets up, turns toward the door, stops) You know when I have to leave for the office. (She shoves a cereal box across the counter toward him) I said forget it; you know I hate cold cereal and instant coffee. Besides, my stomach's in knots anyway. (She shrugs, wordlessly) Have a good day, if you can. (He heads toward the door)

SHE: Give her my love too!

HE: Her . . . her? Oh, for crying out loud.

°   °   °

Can you count the fouls, on either or both sides, in this little domestic interchange. Foul on her, suspicion and accu-

73

sation. Foul on him, personal attack. Foul two for her, silent withdrawal and noncooperation. Foul again for him, nagging, judgment, walk out. Final foul for her, a knee to the emotional groin.

o   o   o

It's "foul play" to criticize the unchangeable. To strike a blow at something that the other cannot change — an in-law or a relative, an event in the past, an inability to measure up to some imaginary ideal, a circumstance of tragedy that could not be helped — even an unusual physical characteristic. It is much more responsible to work at the problems each has created for the other.

It is "foul play" to drag in other issues which injure or anger another beyond reason (becoming hysterical); to confuse your opponent with more than one fight at a time (becoming historical); to bring up items of conflict that have nothing to do with the matter at hand (becoming diversionary). Each must focus on the central problem and one issue at a time, and not drag in additional items to smoke screen the battlefield.

It is "foul play" to attack another in public, or in front of persons who inhibit free and honest interchange. To argue publicly over a private matter is an unfair strategy for silencing the opposition.

It is "foul play" to go for a well-known weak spot in the other — the Achilles' heel — and to use that painful hold to achieve an end totally unrelated to its own significance. Avoid old sores: they add all kinds of confusion to a conflict.

It is "foul play" to rerun an old argument that has been settled and supposedly forgotten as a means of avoiding the present disagreement. Some couples patch up their old quarrels until they are as good as new, and then use them all over again. It's equally foul to allude to old quarrels in subtle jabs at any time for any reason. The grave of a dying relationship is dug by little digs. Let the past be the past.

It is "foul play" to ridicule when there is no reason for disrespect; to exaggerate with the bitter word "always" or to add any intentional overstatement; to threaten with violence as a cover-up for your own weakness; to withhold another's actual rights to gain something outside your rights; to bargain with sex, money, the children, or any other tool for manipulating or using the other person.

Only when we become afraid of being bested one more time will we resort to foul tactics. And that may include each of us, at times. Until we learn to fight fairly by putting first values first.

The goal of conflict in marriage is not to end in a knock-out (either technical or actual). The goal is to end in a clinch. Conflict only ends when it results in togetherness, understanding, reconciliation, and deepening intimacy.

o   o   o

Resolving conflict creatively is the result of love-in-action. Love is something you do. It must be expressed in all three levels of communication: the verbal (I love you), the nonverbal (I feel with you, I truly hear you), and the symbolic (I give to you).

Love is acting in an understanding way toward the other, whether you understand him/her or not.

Love is acting in a concerned, respectful, self-giving way whether you feel emotions of affection at that moment or not.

It is easier to act ourselves into a new way of thinking than it is to think ourselves into a new way of acting. New thoughts about being kind, understanding, forgiving, so often produce just so many good intentions. The mind doesn't do so well in changing such things. The mind is that faculty we use to find a reason for what the heart — the will — wants to do.

If you want to live in love — then you must take the Jesus-way, by making a decision of your will *to act lovingly*.

This unhesitating love which Jesus taught and lived gives acceptance to the other whether he/she is abrasive or not, friction-causing or not, irritating or not.

It looks for the best in others and recognizes it when it is present.

As Paul describes it:

Love is very patient and kind, never jealous or envious, never boastful nor proud, never haughty or selfish nor rude. Love does not demand its own way. It is not irritable or touchy. It does not hold grudges and will hardly even notice when others do it wrong. It is never glad about injustice, but rejoices whenever truth wins out. If you love someone you will be loyal to him no matter what the cost. You will always believe in him, always expect the best of him, and always stand your ground in defending him (1 Cor. 13:4-7).

Or elsewhere he writes:

Don't be selfish; don't live to make a good impression on others. Be humble, thinking of others as better than yourself. Don't just think about your own affairs, but be interested in others too and in what they are doing (Phil. 2:3, 4).

Or again he suggests:

Don't just pretend that you love others; really love them. Hate what is wrong. Stand on the side of the good. Love each other with brotherly affection and take delight in honoring each other (Rom. 12:9, 10). [17]

All these are things you first do — then feel. First we must act in love — then love will act through us.

And that, of course, is love — the Jesus' kind of love that reaches out to give acceptance to others, no matter whether they seem lovable at the moment of conflict.

Love adjusts its behavior to others as they are. Not always agreeing, but accepting them anyway.

Love assumes the best motives are present in others. It does not judge the other's motives by assigning the worst known to man.

Love believes the best of others, not comparing their weak points with our strong points.

Love makes allowance for others' eccentricities; it can afford to forget oddities in order to affirm others as persons.

Love bears with other people's ill humors, overlooks their thoughtless blunders, and forgives any insults or personal attack.

Love is something you do, then something you become, and at last, it's something you are.

CHAPTER SIX

To Be Sexual Means . . .

He mutters some barely audible, unintelligible sounds, climbs out of bed, fumbles into his robe, tells the woodwork that he just can't sleep, and clumps downstairs to the family room.

As his footsteps fade, she begins to breathe again. She doesn't want him to know she's heard. As if she were sleeping. Sleeping! Fat chance. After their clash has just brought all communication to a halt.

In the family room, he switches on the tube, clicks across the channels looking for something to stop his thinking. No luck. The first sexy model on a talk show snaps it all back in focus. She's pushed him away again. And expects him to turn off just like that! Love? No love around here.

She rolls over, punches the pillow into imaginary softness, tries to shut out the TV sounds that come drifting up the stairs. Tries harder to shut off the resentment that keeps firing her feelings.

"This is the umpteenth time she's done it. She's backed me away every time this month. Cold look, cold shrug, cold shoulder! So women are slow starters, this one's a no-starter. And the excuses, I've heard 'em all!"

She fights tears now. "But what could I say, tell him I'm too tired? It's late, I've got a headache, and tomorrow's gonna be a big day? No, excuses only get him angry. I had to tell him. Straight. Unless he shows a little affection at other times, he can forget the crash warm-up for sex. It turns me off."

"Turned off? She's turned off all right — all the way off as far as I'm concerned. Of all the girls in my life, I had to pick a lemon. It wasn't always this way . . . but lately, what's getting to her?"

"If he only showed some understanding, a little affection some other way, I think I could respond. But this way it's not love! I feel numb and dead inside. I don't feel anything anymore."

"I'll fix her clock. Give her a dig in front of her friends. Next party we're at and she's dressed fit to kill, I'll rub it in. 'All that advertising and no sale?' I'll ask. 'I answer the ad and all I get are rain checks.' "

"If I felt he really accepted me, I'd be open to love-making, I guess. But he doesn't really love me. Sometimes I think it shows to others, and I wonder what they're thinking. . . ."

o   o   o

When people say they have a serious problem of sexual adjustment in marriage, they do have a problem. But seldom is the problem sex. A shortage of acceptance, perhaps, and a loss of trust. But not really sex.

o   o   o

When a marriage is seriously disturbed, sexual maladjustment is almost always a factor. But it is almost never the only problem, or even the primary problem.

o o o

When a man says, "She's 100 percent female until 9:15 p.m., then she's suddenly neuter," he's likely placing the blame in the wrong place. It's not her femininity that's at fault, it's their maturity. Or the lack of maturing affection between them.

Every married man, every married woman needs and desires a unifying experience of sexual completion with the other. But when the price is too high, each will avoid the other's advances. Not because of an absence of need or desire, but because something has gone wrong. When sex has become a hurting experience, it is evaded. The hurt most often arises from a lack of emotional-spiritual acceptance which makes sexual acceptance an outrage of the person's integrity.

o o o

Not all sex, within marriage, is good.

Both rape and prostitution can occur in marriage. The man who threatens or even abuses his wife to force sexual intercourse is committing rape. The woman who uses sex to manipulate her husband is committing prostitution — even if her price is a new hat instead of the $50 a night demanded by a "professional." [18]

Sex in marriage is good when it is mutually willed, mutually controlled, and exercised in mutual agreement. "A wife dare not ration her husband . . . nor dare she use sex as a prize or an award. Probably these two negative approaches drive more men away from their wives than any other reason." [19]

Paul gives insightful help on mutual sharing in sexual matters:

The husband should give his wife what is due to her as his wife, and the wife should be as fair to her husband. The wife has no longer full rights over her own person, but shares them with her husband. In the same way the husband shares his personal rights with his wife. Do not cheat each other of normal sexual intercourse, unless of course you both decide to abstain temporarily to make special opportunity for fasting and prayer. But afterward you should resume relations as before, or you will expose yourselves to the obvious temptation of the devil (1 Cor. 7:3-5).

o   o   o

Whatever problems a marriage encounters — money, in-laws, differences in values, conflicts in personality, variations in taste — counselors once saw them all as rooted in sexual maladjustment. New insights have tended to reverse many of their verdicts. Conflicts in sexual adjustment are more often the symptoms of deeper emotional pain than the cause of it all.

David R. Mace, the dean of American Marriage Counselors, says: "Sexual maladjustment in itself is very seldom a basic problem between two people. We find that it is almost always a manifestation of deeper emotional maladjustment. One of the individuals is not comfortable about his or her sexuality, or what they as a couple have to express to each other is so devious and twisted that sex won't work for them. This is true of such things as impotence and frigidity."[20]

The real problem is often evidenced in an accompanying inability or disinterest in communicating, or in a stubborn refusal to trust each other. So the tensions of suspicion and fear become barriers to normal sexual fulfillment.

o   o   o

The gap between a couple's statement of feeling or fact and their actual inner fears may be so great that they are unable to bring the two together in discussion.

Aloud he might say, if he dared, "It's really her fault.

If she cared at all, she'd want me just like I want her. She's becoming more cold and distant all the time. Why can't she feel what I feel?"

But inside he wonders, "What's wrong with me that I can't awaken her feelings of sexual response? Why do I keep failing her? Am I not a man?"

Aloud she might say, if she could, "It's all his fault. If he really loved me, he'd know what I need. But all he's interested in is himself and his own fantasies. He doesn't help me to feel a thing."

Inside she wonders, "Am I frigid? I should be able to respond to him somehow. But the harder he tries, the more I feel that he doesn't care about me, just my bed and body."

The problem may be hidden behind a very self-righteous front. Sexual conflicts are sternly repressed and concealed behind very proper and often pious words.

Such a wife may say:

"I have borne his sexual demands, suffered his ruttish behavior."

"He can't say I turned him away."

"I bore him five children without a complaint."

"I have never once refused him in nineteen years of marriage; it's my sacred marital duty as a wife."

"I've given him the best years of my life with so little love in return. . . ."

Or such a husband may insist:

"She's almost always too tired at bedtime, so I let her alone like she says."

"I guess she knows that when she's got me to the point where I really need her, I'll settle for any little part she's willing to give."

"I give her everything she could want, I can't see why she doesn't respect me."

"I help around the house in all my spare time, I always do dishes, I carry my share of the load with the kids."

o   o   o

In these deadlocks of sexual maladjustment, most couples assume the way out is to do what they've been doing only do it a bit better. "If I only try a little harder," they tell themselves, "maybe I'll hit on the magic combination." So the man who tries and fails, tries harder and fails more painfully. The self-sacrificial wife sacrifices herself more completely, tells herself how holy and noble it is, gets some satisfaction from the righteous feelings, but only hurts both herself and her husband the more.

If there is any hope of healing, it must come through a readjustment. They need new insights, new understandings of themselves and each other. They must develop a new desire each to assist the other in becoming the whole person emotionally, spiritually, and sexually which he or she could be.

Assistance through counseling can be extremely important. A husband and wife should assure one another that whenever either feels that outside help is needed, both will consent to go to a qualified counselor.

Often the husband jeers, "You mean you'd go to talk to a minister/doctor/counselor about that?" Or he may feel threatened and say, "Don't you dare tell any of our intimate secrets to anybody — or else!"

But it is perfectly in order and extremely common for a marriage to need a referee, or such objective viewpoints as a disinterested third party may offer.

Recently a gifted, happily married, seemingly well-adjusted couple — he a college professor, she a nurse — went to a marriage counselor. Acquaintances were astonished. "Why you?" they asked. "We thought you were perfectly adjusted."

"We're happy enough," they replied. "It's just that we discovered we were talking past each other on a very important issue; we couldn't discover why, and we didn't want it to develop into anything."

That is the wisdom of experience. But if you're still afraid to go outside for help, can't you begin on your own to help each other?

Perhaps you can begin by getting at your own understandings of the meanings of sex to each other. Compare them to some of the meanings of sex to the mature man and wife which we explore next. Don't be afraid if the conversation starts off slowly.

o   o   o

HE: Honey, do you enjoy being a wife. . . .
SHE: That's some silly question. Of course I do. . . .
HE: I mean, do you enjoy being a wife to me. . . in. . . .
SHE: . . . in . . . what?
HE: . . . in . . . sex.
SHE: John! For goodness sake!
HE: Why the outrage? What's wrong with discussing sex?
SHE: It's not something to talk about.
HE: Oh, you mean, it's something it's all right to do if the lights are out, the covers up?
SHE: No, it's just the words, the idea of talking about it. It's. . . .
HE: Embarrassing?
SHE: Kind of . . . but I guess it just makes me uncomfortable. I think talking would spoil it.
HE: You mean like it's sacred and holy and all that?
SHE: Not exactly. I mean like, isn't it better to just be ourselves and not try to explain what happens when we're together?
HE: I don't want to explain it . . . it's just . . . well. . . .
SHE: Just what?
HE: I feel like I fail you.
SHE: You do? It's not you. If anyone fails, it's me.

HE: See? That's why we need to talk. To find out what it
       means to each other, and to be sure it really does
       mean something? See?

SHE: Uh-huh . . . I think I see. But I'm scared.

o   o   o

"He who made us
from the beginning
Made us male and female."
Sexual.
It is good.
It is of God.

o   o   o

Sex is celebration.

Sex celebrates the union of two selves into one whole relationship. Sex celebrates the fulfillment of two persons' sexuality, each in the other. Sex celebrates the completion of love's opening of one self to another in unconditional acceptance.

Celebration, meaning "the joyous recognition of worth," is essentially worship. Is sex worship? "Sex is a sacrament," say many thinkers, "a sacrament meaning that sex is a physical expression of a spiritual reality, an outward and visible sign of an inward and spiritual grace." A form of worship? Why not?

But if sex is worship, it is not the worship of sex. Sex is not God. Only the living God is worthy of our complete devotion, service, and loyalty. When sex seizes first place in life, it is an idol to be smashed.

Sex is worship, as it symbolizes in the man-woman relationship what the true nature of the human-God relationship is intended to be. The Bible, with no embarrassment or hesitation, uses the human experience of sexuality to reveal the true nature of man's covenant and union with

85

God. To begin, it declares human sexuality is a part of the image of God in man.

> God created man
> In His own image.
> In the image of God,
> He created him;
> Male and female
> He created them.

"God and man are related," said Hosea, Jeremiah, Ezekiel, and other of the prophets, "as husband and wife." The Apostle Paul explained it further (Ephesians 5:21-23) and John the Revelator celebrated it:

> Then I saw a new Heaven and a new earth, for the first Heaven and the first earth had disappeared, and the sea was no more. I saw the holy city, the new Jerusalem, descending from God out of Heaven, prepared as a bride dressed in beauty for her husband. Then I heard a great voice from the throne crying:
> "See! The home of God is with men and he will live among them. They shall be his people, and God himself shall be with them, and will wipe away every tear from their eyes. Death shall be no more, and never again shall there be sorrow or crying or pain. For all those former things are past and gone" (Rev. 21:1-4).

The biblical phrase for describing man-woman inter-sexuality is "to know." This is not a squeamish evasion of the realities of sex, but a profound understanding of the true nature of sexual unity. And the identical words are used in God's invitation for man to enter into a "knowing" relationship with Him. To the Hebrew "to know" meant a spiritual, physical, and joyful sexual experience of two lives made one. Genesis 4:1, 25; Matthew 1:24, 25.

Sexual unity between man and woman, when it is an unconditional covenant of love and loyalty, is a visible expression of God's covenant-way with man. In such a setting, sex is celebration. It is even worship.

o   o   o

Sex is celebration of creation.

As created people we do not exist as individuals. We are not meant to be individuals. We are persons. We are designed for relationship, incomplete in isolation. We cannot recognize ourselves without others; we cannot truly know ourselves except in relation to another. Sex is a celebration of God's dual creation, man-woman.

Sexuality is also our celebration of God's continuing creativity. God has chosen to mediate His creative activity in the conception of new persons through the intimate act of love-union. He has honored the simple act of joining bodies with the ultimate significance of beginning life.

Two who give themselves to each other in the intimacy of marriage, celebrate the eternal potential of their act of love. This awareness of its creative meaning gives character to sexual union even when it is meant as an act of joyous communion with no intention of conception. Then, too, it is a celebration of His creation.

o   o   o

Sex is celebration of love.

"Even though it should be quite obvious, it often goes unmentioned in Christian circles that the sex act itself is perhaps the highest and most concentrated expression of love humanly possible. In no other single act is man's entire being so thoroughly embodied; no other act comes so close to the losing of oneself in the unity of two persons." [21]

Love is a constant, willed concern for the other person and for the wholeness of that person.

Loving concern asks: "What is Nancy's good? What is, or will continue to be, wholeness for her? Do I genuinely want that for her? What can I do that will assist Nancy's pilgrimage to the holy wholeness of her own unique identity?" And loving concern asks of Nancy: "What expressions of love will release David to become the man he can fully be? What response will release him to discover love for a woman who is wholly woman?"

So charm and gentleness (femininity) is blended with solidness and strength (masculinity) in the mutual concern of love. In the mutual self-giving of sex we celebrate this intimate, self-forgetful sharing in which each releases the other to fully "know," to truly love. In "the wonder of recognition" each discovers the other in open-armed acceptance, and in the other each discovers him/her self.

° ° °

Sex is celebration of joy.

Sexuality is good; the full, true expression of it is joyful, natural, and playful. But sex can be taken too seriously, either in the piety of observing it as sacrament, or in the perspiration caused by the prophets of technique who turn people into worried performers. Then it loses the joyful exuberance of two persons "pouring forth life in an aimless joyful series of words, movements, and actions."

These quoted words are lifted from Romano Guardini's book, *The Spirit of Liturgy*, in which he argued that liturgy and worship should not be mysterious and austere but free, spontaneous, and joyful like the play of a child.

> The child, when it plays, does not aim at anything. It has no purpose but to exercise its youthful powers, to pour forth its life in an aimless series of movements, words, and actions . . . all of which is purposeless, but full of meaning nevertheless. . . . That is what play means; it is life, pouring itself forth without aim. [22]

These words on the free expression of joy in worship are equally applicable to the expression of joy in marriage through sexual relationship. So much emphasis has been placed on the "how to," so much pressure has been exerted on simultaneous experience, that many partners lose the sense of sex as joy and play, as an end in itself. They become "little old technicians." [23]

Sex becomes something to accomplish, an act to be perfectly performed to prove masculinity or femininity. Or they may see sexual adjustment as the means to a stable marriage on which the other successes of the future depend. It becomes work, not play. A labor of love, not a "pouring forth of joyful meaning."

Sex can only be such a free act of joy when it occurs inside the complete freedom of loving security called marriage. It is almost impossible for two persons to experience such a liberty to let-go-of-the-self in spontaneous joy without the mutual trust of long and constant contact with each other. Contact that is secure, responsible, and with the promise of permanence.

o   o   o

Sex is celebration of fidelity.

"Marriage is based not so much on love as on fidelity," the late Swiss theologian Emil Brunner wrote.

Fidelity gives substance to a marriage. It guarantees exclusiveness which says, "Your love is so valuable, so all-satisfying to me that I voluntarily keep myself only for you." It offers permanence which affirms: "Whatever change or alteration may come to you, my love will be constant. I will be yours, through good or ill."

Celebration of fidelity gives incomparable beauty to sexual give and take.

William Hamilton, in his book *Faith, Sex and Love* expresses this poignantly:

> The first sexual experience is so overwhelming and different from any other experience that it had better be preserved as a means of symbolizing and giving power and meaning to mar-

riage. . . . I am bound in an indelible and permanent way to the first woman who shows me who I am and what it is to be a man. . . . One of the real ways a couple learns to trust one another, to come together, to forgive and to understand, is by sharing each other's sexual mistakes, fears, and hopes. Sexual innocence at first, gradually transformed by gentle experiments and experience — this is a forger of a unity that never lets the old loneliness return. [24]

Sex is celebration only when the participants share a common past, experience a common present, and anticipate a common future. And this is called marriage.

CHAPTER SEVEN

Who Leads in the Home?

A PARABLE

"Father," a son said, "Gertrude and I wish to marry. May we have your blessing?"

"You will have my blessing," the father replied, "if you can tell me who will have the authority in your home."

"I will, of course," the son instantly replied.

"I doubt it," the father answered. "In fact, I question whether you can name more than one family in this whole community that is not controlled by the woman."

"That is not true," the son replied, "why. . . ."

"I'll put it to the test," the father wagered. "I'll give you ten hens and two horses. You may select any ten homes. Go and question them. If the wife rules the roost, give them a hen. If the husband pulls the most weight, give them a horse. I wager you'll still have the team of horses to use for your own."

The son selected the ten homes, loaded the crate of hens on the wagon, hitched the horses, and began his investigation. Evening found him at the tenth home, still holding two horses and the last chicken.

"Who exercises the authority in this home?" he asked.

"I do," the husband replied.

"Always?"

"Always!"

"Is this true?" he asked the wife.

"It is always true," she replied obediently.

"Then one of the horses is yours," he said. "Which will it be?"

"I'll take the white one," the man said instantly. "I've always wanted a snow-white horse."

"Now, Joe," the wife cautioned, "think through it a little more. If you took the black one, you could team her with old Ben and you'd have a matched team."

"Um . . . right, I'll take a black one," the husband said.

"Huh-uh . . . wrong," the boy replied. "You'll take the hen."

o o o

Does this old German anecdote give any insight into the traditional nature of German family structures? Contrary to this oft-told story, were not the fathers invariably given a dominant role of authority, the mothers an inferior position of submissiveness and obedience? The story may simply reveal that humor served as a means of enforcing male-supremacy doctrine.

Or does it confess in humor that even in the rigidly patriarchal family, leadership may be truly expressed by the person given the lesser place? Then, he who insists on "superiority" becomes not a leader, but a censor. Decisions are not made by such persons, they are simply ratified. He passes approval on the more intuitive suggestion of the other, and then vainly congratulates himself on holding the "power."

o   o   o

What is leadership in the home?

There is the "man-is-and-ever-shall-be-the-sole-leader" theory. This view assumes that some superior gift of chromosomes and hormones makes man the natural possessor of unique talents and abilities which fit him to lead out. He is, due to his strength, size, intelligence, and tendency toward dominance, naturally "the boss."

Dominance may effectively give orders and demand control, but it does not lead. Dominant authority serves well as a censor, an enforcer of views, a dispenser of discipline. But that is not leading.

And dominance is not uniquely characteristic of either sex. It is often an evidence of a rigid, authoritative personality. Frequently it is a sign of weakness and insecurity, indicating that the domineering person fears change or challenge so greatly that he/she cannot risk being flexible and is terrified of becoming vulnerable before another personality.

There is the "husband-is-the-head-and-the-head-is-the-leader" theory. The husband may be the "head," but to be head and to be leader are two different things. Headmanship is not synonymous with leadership. The headman may serve as the formal "chief-in-charge," as the recognized "legal name and nominal head" (as does the husband, whose family name becomes the title for social use). But such "headmanship" is much more than a matter of status, rank, or recognition. It accepts the responsibility for failures and successes in the relationship, but does not assume sole authority in decisions and directions.

Nor does the biblical recognition of man as "head" in

marriage endow him with authority and right-to-dominate. Some have thought that Paul's patterning of man's role as "head" after Christ's position as "Head-to-the-church" gives great weight to the husband's role.

Does the husband, like Christ, become Lord and Master? The ultimate word? Since the two, man and Christ, are compared, does that give man all the rights and roles of Lord in the home? On the contrary, the purposes of the comparison are specifically stated in both 1 Corinthians 11:1-10, and Ephesians 5:21-33." Headship means responsibility and initiative. Responsibility to act in love. Initiative to act in service. As Christ acted in self-giving love, and self-humbling service (giving us a whole new meaning to "headship"), so husbands take the initiative in building an atmosphere of loving, self-sacrificing service.

Headmanship is only part of leadership, one facet of one kind of leadership.

Christ cut through our contorted ideas of headship with surgical words:

> Among the heathen it is their kings who lord it over them, and their rulers are given the title of 'benefactors.' But it must not be so with you! *Your* greatest man must become like a junior and your leader must be a servant. Who is the greater, the man who sits down to dinner or the man who serves him? Obviously, the man who sits down to dinner — yet *I* am the one who is the servant among you (Lk. 22:25-27).

o   o   o

What then is leadership? If it is not something a person is, then it must be something he or she does.

Leadership is accepting responsibilities and performing certain functions in a marriage relationship in a way that advances both persons together toward their goals.

If leadership is "doing certain tasks or functions," then it is obviously not a certain role, a certain sex, or a permanent possession of one of the persons. Leadership alternates; it is a contribution made by either or both together.

If leadership is "helping and serving so that both move forward," then it is an action done by either person in a way that liberates both. It may go unnoticed. It happens best when unrecognized. It is accepted most easily when it is unself-conscious, selfless, self-giving. When it is exercised in the Christ-way of giving help.

Helping another is best defined as giving another the freedom to change, and to change voluntarily. This is a creative exercise in leadership. In contrast, authoritarian dominance prohibits free choice, and inhibits free interchange and the freedom to change.

o   o   o

The autocratic personality	The Christ-ocratic personality
gives orders without asking questions, without permitting questions;	asks questions, seeks to truly hear, suggests alternatives;
makes demands, dishes out directives, lays down the law, defensive if challenged.	respects freedom and dignity of others, can affirm the truth clearly and concretely, but nondefensively.
requires compliance regardless of consent or agreement.	values willing cooperation works for open agreement and understanding.
pushes and manipulates one-man rule in over-under position.	leads, attracts, persuades personal relationships in side-by-side identification.
says "you do, you must do, you ought to have done, you'd better do."	says "come, let's do, we might have done, can we try?"

depends on his own external authority to motivate others.	depends on their internal integrity to motivate them.
generates friction, resistance, and resentment.	generates acceptance, cooperation, and reconciliation.
separates and isolates people.	unites and helps persons relate to each other. [25]

o   o   o

A person tends to be like the people with whom he works, plays, and lives. He tends to absorb the qualities of those who lead.

Marriage partners tend to become like each other, taking on the other's qualities, or developing the opposite characteristics in negative reaction to the other.

Leadership shared in mutual respect can establish a climate of dignity, freedom, and responsibility, creating an atmosphere which is comforting and stimulating to both. A Christian atmosphere. In it, each is free to grow toward personal maturity and each is eager to see the shape of Christ forming in the other. See Galatians 4:19, 20.

But where one seizes power, or both struggle for control, an atmosphere of competition and conflict chokes communication and understanding. Even (or) the unconscious assuming power by one partner or the other will mold the relationship, perhaps in ways neither desire.

o   o   o

HE: Why don't you speak out and say what you think?
SHE: What's the use?
HE: What do you mean, "What's the use?" I hear you.
SHE: I know . . . but then you go ahead and make the decisions anyway.

HE: Isn't that what you want? You always say . . . "Well, you decide." Then when I do, you aren't happy.

SHE: Well, sometimes I disagree.

HE: You disagree afterward. Why can't you tell me how you feel beforehand? Are you too weak to come out with it?

SHE: So that's it; you think I'm weak.

HE: Well . . . sometimes. . . .

SHE: How else can I be, with you taking such a strong-hand? . . .

HE: If I didn't decide things, they'd never get decided. I've got to be strong. You force me to be that way.

SHE: How do I force you?

HE: By acting so weak.

SHE: Look, I've discovered something. I'm not so silent. I'm . . . I'm my old self with some people, where I feel accepted for what I am. But I feel so put down when I'm with you.

HE: Why can't you just be the same, all the time, like me?

SHE: Like you? You're not the same. When you're with your brother-in-law, the doctor, you're more silent — "weak" you call it. But when you're with my brother, you're high and mighty.

HE: You mean, sometimes I'm weak, sometimes strong?

SHE: Right.

HE: And it depends on how I feel about the people I'm with, like if they're above me or . . .?

SHE: Yes.

HE: And you think that's how it is with us?

SHE: Isn't it? If you say I'm always weak, it must be.

HE: And you think I make you that way?

SHE: No, it's just that you . . . well, you've always got the last word on things. You're usually right. I've got no chance to express myself. Oh, I'm talking too much. Forget it.

97

HE: No, that's what I've been doing. Maybe it's time we tried something else to make sure we're being open to each other.

o   o   o

A "strong" husband may choose a wife whom he can dominate. He resents competition or contradiction. He wants a submissive, compliant mate. As years pass, he may come to resent her submissiveness as a sign of weakness.

Or a dominant wife may choose a man she can "mother." Instead, she smothers. He, tiring of it all, attempts to express his true feelings, only to be beaten down with a word or two. She cannot respect a man who is flattened with one swat. He cannot respond to a woman who clips him when he opens his true feelings. So hostility, morbidity, and often infidelity follow.

o   o   o

Negotiating the responsibilities and the unique ways each person prefers to perform is a marriage-long task. They cannot be negotiated once, then forgotten. People mature, grow, and change. The experiences of life, delightful or difficult, either fit or unfit them to continue interacting in the same ways.

If she married him to fulfill her father's role in her life, her expectations will be a major factor in negotiating their life-style at the time of marriage. Three years of maturing may release her from the father need, to a great extent. Her relationship with her husband can now develop on a totally different base.

If he married her to fulfill the "mother-was-a-good-servant" role of maid, laundress, housewife, and to perform these in silent efficiency, he may later discover that she is a person to be respected as the person she is. Their relationship can begin over again — if new negotiation is possible.

Marriage relationships must each achieve their own balance through honest, fair negotiation. They can maintain that balance only through repeated negotiations. But through it all, certain things do remain constant.

Leadership is a function which should always be shared.

Authority in one area or another is a responsibility which is mutually designated to one or the other through honest negotiation. It can be renegotiated at any time.

Responsibility is delegated by both — to each other. Two people may early work their way through such a division of labor in general terms and may even continue to fulfill the same tasks and roles throughout life. But not necessarily so.

Changes come in work, health, schedule, family, outside responsibilities, and many other areas that call for new negotiations and usually a new division of responsibilities.

If one partner is uncomfortable with the way the relationship is being played out, he/she has a right to blow the whistle and call for a new toss-up. Often this means calling in a referee to clarify the situation.

The referee role cannot be played by any spectator. They quickly take sides, or worse yet, alternate sides as the story unfolds. A counselor is needed who will neither believe nor disbelieve either, but will bring objectivity into the situation and uncover the true feelings of each.

If the relationship is off balance, if one has assumed a primary role at the expense of the other's integrity, then a new set of ground rules will need to be drawn up.

If the isolation of being housebound is driving a wife to distraction, she has every right to express her creativity in work outside the home — provided responsible decisions are made in respect for all the needs of the children.

If a man's work is demanding a lion's share of his time,

and the children are growing up with virtually no opportunity to know their father, the wife has a right to call for a reapportionment of his time according to their family's actual values.

If there is conflict of roles, either person who is feeling the pinch has the right to call for open negotiations. If the wife is convinced she must leave the first move to her man, she may wait forever before he recognizes that their lifestyle is shortchanging her and cutting her off from relationships with others, from meaningful work, and from a sense of fulfillment.

Life together is life shared. Shared love, shared work, shared opportunities, shared leadership, even shared initiative. Man, the nominal head, may function officially for both in public matters of leadership. Woman, recognized as his equal in partnership, leads with, and not against him. Together, they choose to grow.

CHAPTER EIGHT

The Meaning of Money . . .

In the beginning the man took unto himself a wife. And lo, they did live happily, even unto the thirty-first day, when many charge accounts rained upon him, yea, as in a flood.

For lo, though the husband did make sufficient bread to keep body and soul together, yet had the wiles of the spoiler ensnared the wife, calling forth grievous wants from her breast. Color television, myriad appliances, and innumerable credit card purchases had multiplied fruitfully, which came nigh unto sinking the ship of matrimony. For the winds of inflation blew upon the land, and each one lusted after his neighbor's goods. And the man was sorely angered and spoke forth bitter words, from which his wife took great sorrow, but not unto repentance. For upon the first day of the week she went forth again and spent abundantly.

Then it was that the man was sorely pressed, and he took unto himself a second labor by the light of the moon, and his wife likewise, and their lives did pass like ships in the night. Behold, the time of the paying of bills returneth, and the man saith unto his wife, "Yea, though I moonlight and work my fingers to the bone, I canst not get ahead of thee!" And his wife beateth her breast. "Truly," she saith, "I am now filled with remorse. Let my bed be empty if I mend not my ways."

Then gave she ear unto her husband and they took counsel together that they might be of one mind in their values, and beat the system, yea, and buildeth for their future according to a budget. And so did they walk prudently before the Lord, who knoweth our ways and pitieth those who cannot make ends meet. [26]

o   o   o

HE: Look, honey, I've got it figured out.

SHE: I don't want to hear about it.

HE: Now you've got to hear about it. We can buy this hot racing rig I've been telling you about, and when we win. . . .

SHE: If we win, you mean.

HE: *When* we win we'll have all our investment back, and then we'll be in the money. Now I've got this three-day option on it.

SHE: You took an option on it?

HE: Sure — and the way it adds up is — we only have to find nine thousand.

SHE: Nine thousand!

HE: Easy, we can get a six-thousand-dollar mortgage on the house, and you've got three thousand from your old man's estate.

SHE: You want to blow the money I got from my family?

HE: No . . . invest it, honey. It's a sure thing. And you know how much racing would mean to me. . . .

SHE: Yeah, sure I know. It would take you away from us

every available minute — and then break your fool neck in the end.

HE: Now, looky here (voice held even with controlled anger). This is our chance to live, our chance to get in on the fun, in on the money.

SHE: Dreams. Air castles. You'll ruin everything we've got. (She exits, leaving for her job. He sits hunched over his figures, musing to himself.)

HE: Doesn't a man have the right to follow his dream? Don't all dreams involve a little risk? Sure, the odds on getting rich quick are a little long, but then — look at all the enjoyment, right? And the decision's all mine, not hers. But what about her? I'd be using money that's really hers, at least it's from her dad, and it's her right to say "no." Of course, it is a joint account. And a joint marriage. I can put it all in the rig if I want to. . . . Once it's spent, what can she do? And the option runs out, tomorrow!

o   o   o

Money. To one partner in marriage it may mean security, stability, status; to the other it may signify freedom to spend, to fulfill dreams, to express his true self-image.

Money. In marriage, it has as many meanings as there are mates. Until. Until communication worms its way through the emotional thicket of financial dreams, expectations, habits, values, wants, and needs. Until. Until understanding tears out some of the underbrush of tantalizing attractions, of seductive appeals to consume, of compulsive needs to compete with other couples.

The handling of finances is one of the major emotional battlegrounds of marriage. Seldom because of the lack of finances. Often because of unrealistic and immature money values. More often because money is used as an emotional weapon to control or manipulate each other. Most often because money is utilized as a way of compensating for deep inadequacies.

A man may use money unjustifiably to fulfill himself in a hobby or interest. Even though it means the sacrifice of his wife's and family's hopes and future. Then he'll accuse her of being cold and critical.

A woman may drive her man to succeed, prod him on in amassing wealth to provide the prestige and security she craves. Then she'll reject him for burying himself in his work and avoiding her.

Or a couple may find themselves bound by impossible goals, to achieve through accumulating wealth, or to win acceptance in a select group by collecting their status symbols and placing them on display.

o o o

SHE: I was at Susan's this afternoon.

HE: (Aside) Not again! (Aloud) So! What's new with them?

SHE: Their car.

HE: Car? Not another car!

SHE: You should see it!

HE: What've they come up with this time?

SHE: One of those little sports type jobs with wide wheels, top comes down, a gearshift thing on the floor.

HE: So. What else is new?

SHE: Well, they've just signed the contract for a new pool.

HE: Pool. Next you'll tell me they're installing a complete sauna and health club. Honey, Susan and Bill can play their games of keeping one up on the whole community. If that's what they want of life, OK! But why should we try it? Let them do their thing!

SHE: I'm not saying we should try, but it's getting a little embarrassing being seen in our old car.

HE: Then the car really got to you, did it? But our car

isn't that old yet! Oh, what's the use. Sure, it's no
picnic parking it alongside everyone else's, but if we
can make it till next fall, we'll be a long way ahead,
right? You know we agreed on that.

SHE: By then they'll have another new one.

HE: Great, let 'em have it. We'll pass on this round and
be one ahead.

SHE: I'm not sure you know how it feels.

HE: Don't I? I've felt all the grins, the "how many miles
have you got on that car?" remarks.

SHE: What do you say?

HE: Nothing. If we're going to do what we said we really
want out of life, we'll just have to sacrifice a little
along the way, won't we?

SHE: I suppose. Let them play the game. But it gets to
you. . . .

HE: Yeah. It sure does. But we can live with it, right?

SHE: Right!

o   o   o

Open account books — open to each other.

Mutual decision-making — shared with each other.

Common life-values — agreed upon together.

Long-term goals — that choose a life-style worthy of
your life together.

These are the crucial elements in handling family
finances.

Open books to each other. One of the easiest ways to
create problems for each other is withholding information.
When partners refuse to confide matters that are important
to both, then all sorts of misunderstandings spring up.

"My husband always tells me he's got plenty of money,"
the wife of a small businessman told me. "I ask for some
cash, he tells me to look the other way, and then pulls it
out of some hiding place in his office. Tells me he's got all

the money I ever need stashed away, but he's kinda tight with it."

Strange things may happen in a marriage like this. If he keeps her in total ignorance on their money matters, she may see him as a money tree, available for a shakedown at any moment of want. She believes he will buy her anything — within reasonable limits — that she may ask. But she carefully avoids testing that assumption. If the day comes that he goes broke, she may be shocked to meet a loan officer at the door officially repossessing her new sports coupe.

Withholding information, though it may be called "saving her a lot of worries," sets the stage for conflicts that may become terminal. It is important for each to be aware of what money represents psychically and emotionally to the other. If money has hidden meanings — as it usually does — it can touch off complications beyond imagining.

•   •   •

HE: But honey, you remember we agreed. . . .

SHE: (Defensive) Agreed to what?

HE: We agreed you would bank all your salary for a rainy day — and this is it. We need a new furnace.

SHE: Blow it on a furnace? We didn't agree on that!

HE: Now honey, you remember we agreed to live on my salary, and save yours for an emergency — or luxury.

SHE: You're not going to touch it!

HE: Of course I'm not; I can't. But you're going to draw out fifteen hundred to rework our heating system.

SHE: Oh, no — you can get a loan.

HE: (He flips his top) And pay all that interest?! You've got to be kidding! That's fiscal irresponsibility.

SHE: Certainly we can discuss this without arguing. With all this heat, we don't need a furnace.

HE: I'm sorry, honey. We're two mature people. We've always settled money matters mutually. Can't we do it this time, too?

SHE: "Mutually." We'll mutually agree that you're right — is that it?

HE: No, let's come to mutual agreement on what's right for us both.

SHE: Then we go to Mutual Savings and draw out my money, is that it?

HE: Well . . . let's go over the budget together first, OK?

o   o   o

To him, money is usable, savable, spendable, a mutual asset.

To her, money is independence. It is a security that guarantees independence. It is the storehouse of protection she relies on should her life of interdependence with him suddenly end or slowly wane.

Two such totally different attitudes toward money need to come together. Their different meanings for money need to be explained. In a meeting of meaning. Communication it's called.

o   o   o

For the maturing person, money is simply a medium of exchange. Money is time turned into exchangeable, usable, tradable form through work or service. In very practical terms, "money is time." But once a man reverses that to say "time is money," he is in danger of becoming a money slave. He can get caught in the accelerating tailspin of circular thinking we call materialism.

From the view that money is time. . .

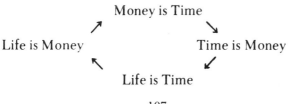

Money is Time

Life is Money   Time is Money

Life is Time

. . . he circles all the way to the conclusion that "life is money."

From here on the equations multiply. Money is status, money is power, money is success, money is beauty, money is sex appeal. Money is everything.

What does money really mean to your husband or wife?

Only open books, open attitudes, open understandings of each other's values and open goals can bring clear-headedness to marriage relationships.

o   o   o

SHE: Harry, what's that you're looking at, Harry? Not another thing on cars. Where is this going to stop?

HE: Let me alone, Helen. So I like cars a little, so what?

SHE: So you like cars, Harry. You must hate 'em. No sooner do we get used to one than you're trading off.

HE: Trading up, Helen, not off. So I like a nice car?

SHE: We've got to talk about this, Harry. You're spending us right out of any chance at security.

HE: Security, securities. Is that all you have to worry about?

SHE: I've got you, haven't I? And your big spending. Your little-boy show-offishness?

HE: That's enough, Helen.

SHE: All right. All right. So what is it this time?

HE: I've decided it should be something a little more sporty this time. Wide wheels, bigger engine.

SHE: I don't want to hear about it.

HE: Look, here's a picture. That's us in there together.

SHE: Harry, if we can't make the decisions together, why should you expect us to enjoy it together?

HE: What kind of answer is that? Money decisions, cars, and such are man's matters, women don't worry about things like that.

SHE: Don't we? We worry all right. What kind of footing

108

are we on when we can't even talk about it?

HE: We're all right, I tell you. I earn the right to blow a little money now and then, don't I?

SHE: That's not the issue, is it? Why can't we make decisions together in things like this?

HE: You said yourself you don't care much for cars. Now you want to tell me what I like. . . .

SHE: I just want in on our future. Is that too much to ask?

⁕   ⁕   ⁕

Every couple should have some mutually agreed-upon strategy for handling money and finances. A working scheme, a system of priorities, an outline for their future. More than a budget, it discusses the values you want in life, not just "what" and "how" you buy. It is a working attitude toward life, a common understanding on values and priorities.

What partner actually handles the finances is a matter open to negotiation. Traditionally it is considered a man's prerogative. Actually, there is no reason why this should be so.

Money-handling responsibilities should be delegated to the partner whose skills, training, or temperament best fits the job. The other should be grateful to be relieved of a task which ill suits him or her. Let him or her who finds fulfillment in this role do the work: planning balanced expenditures, making payments, and laying away savings.

Author Ella May Miller offers wise counsel here: "The wife may be the better financier of the two. If she is to manage the budget, let it be his decision for her to do it. I've seen ruined marriages simply because the wife took over of her own accord. Some took over completely, leaving no area of financial responsibility to the husband.

"Regardless of who takes over the writing of checks, paying of bills, etc., it should be a joint venture as you consult together about regular budget spending. As in all other areas, you need honesty and frankness about personal feelings, wants, etc. Control your money. Don't allow money to control you. This is possible as you focus on loyalties and priorities, and take God in as your Partner." [27]

o   o   o

"Give 10 percent.
Save 10 percent.
Live the rest."

This guideline recommended by counselor-author Charlie W. Shedd is a good beginning base for family budgeting. [28] The first rule — to give — is a joyous act of responsible Christian living. Ten percent is a biblical, practical, responsible minimum. A tithe it is called. It is a tenth invested first, in love for God and neighbor. That should be the motive.

For study of this historic practice of the people of God reaching thousands of years into history, examine Genesis 14:20; 28:20-22; Leviticus 27:30-34; Deuteronomy 14:22-27; 26:1-15; Proverbs 3:9; Malachi 3:10; 1 Corinthians 16:2; 2 Corinthians 8:1-15; 9:1-6. Then finish out with Luke 21:1-4.

How's that for responsible sharing?

o   o   o

Above all, when it comes to choosing your values — travel light.

To live well is to live simply. To live simply demands living with less baggage to carry. To "travel light."

In times of crisis the decision is made for us, and traveling light comes more easily. A doctor in the midst of an epidemic lives on a crisis schedule. A family in financial straits lives on a crisis budget. A home in the grip of illness lives on a crisis workload. A community in a time of emergency lives in a crisis mobilization of persons and equipment.

Right now we are living in crisis times. It is time — high time — to travel light. It is time to sort out our values and pare those we keep down to the core.

Life in the seventies is going to call us to hold our property with a light touch. The problem is, our possessions are likely to hold us. The major danger of affluence is its intoxicating influence. The great threat lies not in the things you may possess, but in the things that will possess you.

Jesus recommended holding one's holdings with a touch as light as a whisper. Listen:

> You cannot serve two masters: God and money. For you will hate one and love the other, or else the other way around.
>
> So my counsel is: Don't worry about *things* — food, drink, and clothes. For you already have life and a body — and they are far more important than what to eat and wear. . . . Will all your worries add a single moment to your life?
>
> Don't store up treasures here on earth where they can erode away or may be stolen. Store them in heaven where they will never lose their value, and are safe from thieves. If your profits are in heaven your heart will be there too" (Mt. 6:24, 25, 27, 19:21). [29]

To take Jesus seriously — if you own one coat, what right have you to a second while another human has none? If you own one home, what right have you to another while some families have no housing? If you live too well on ten thousand a year, what use have you for twelve or twenty when millions have almost nothing?

Certainly, we all have ways of rationalizing our own style of life, standard of living, and stock of wealth. But all these rationales will be coming up for question again and again in the seventies — as never before.

When you examine your values in the light of Christ's teaching — hold your wealth with butterfingers. Travel light — and be prepared to travel lighter!

111

CHAPTER NINE

To Be a Parent Means . . .

Wanted.

The vanishing American father.

Whereabouts unknown.

Last seen on the 7:31 commuter headed for his downtown office.

Wearing a business suit and long sideburns.

Carries an attache case and the visible burden of the business world on his shoulders.

He is known to frequent business luncheons, may be found afternoons on the golf course. Is likely to be seen at dinner with a business associate in a steak house or nightclub.

He is wanted by his wife who would like to contact him for an appointment on their next anniversary. And by three children ages 7, 9, and 13 who would like to make his acquaintance. If located, tell him to call home. His wife, his children — God knows — will be glad you did. And God knows how much they need him!

o   o   o

"The case of the vanishing father" is a mystery only to the child. And even there it is not a mystery long. He soon develops his own theories. And his theories, believed long enough, tend to be accepted as fact.

The most critical impact of father's disappearance is upon the children. A boy needs his father around to develop his images of what it means to be a man. To disc. the meanings of work, to sense the significance of relationships in a masculine context of solidity and loyal security. A daughter needs a father to develop her sense of femininity and to learn what to expect of masculinity. Her values will be molded by his presence or absence as well as the son's.

Lacking this, the child comes to assume the absence of the man is the natural order of things. That familial relationships — which will provide much of the pattern for adult communal relating — are not significant to a man. A boy asks, a girl wonders, then he or she draws lasting conclusions from the father's absenteeism.

o   o   o

Mommie. . .
Where's Daddy?
Huh?
Doesn't he like us anymore?
Why does he have to work all the time?
Cant' he even come for supper?
Humh!
We never see him except. . . .
Well, he stopped by tonight to leave his golf clubs and get his bowling ball.
Peggy's daddy takes her to the zoo. . . .
They go bicycling. . . .
I think maybe they even have fun together.
I wish my daddy was a little fun.

o   o   o

113

HE: Oh, by the way, we'll be going to a little elbow bender at the Benson's Friday evening. Sevenish, I believe.

SHE: But that's the evening we're going to Julie's piano recital.

HE: *We* are going?

SHE: No, just me, of course, and then I've got to stop by the school and meet her new teacher.

HE: Now look here, the Benson's are expecting us. Who knows — my promotion, my advancement in the company, my moving up depends on cementing his friendship on the board.

SHE: Sorry, but I won't disappoint Julie again just for some more business politics.

HE: Now listen, business is business. It's my life. It's our living. And kids are kids. Julie will get over it.

SHE: Oh, no. I've sacrificed our kids for the last time. I'm not going to let them down again.

HE: Who is letting them down? It's just that there are more important things than a piano recital.

SHE: Really? Are there more important "things" than children?

HE: Well, it sure takes the "things" I make to pay for everything you and the kids want. So the business has to come in first once in a while.

SHE: If it only did come in first "just once in a while." When did you last spend an evening doing what they want you to do? You know how you've cut them off, and how we've cut off any friendships that didn't fit in with business. We've chased after people who could "help us get ahead." We've been businessed to death — and here's where I quit! I'm going to rejoin the human race.

HE: Hey, I've got no choice. I've got to go to this party.

SHE: Go.

HE: And I can't go alone.

SHE: If you go, you will. (She disappears into the shower where running water drowns his words.)

HE: Boy, does this burn me up. Can't she see this is one party we can't afford to miss? Sure, Julie does deserve a little of my interest. But in piano? Of course, that's what seems to matter to her more than anything else.

          o   o   o

Any man — with any job — in any profession — can be a father, right?

Wrong! Some men — in some professions — with certain jobs — may be able to afford the necessary time; but for many men, fatherhood should be out. Or do you disagree?

Can a working man be a father? The question must be asked. There are so many people rushing to point fingers at working mothers and to lay the blame for juvenile delinquency, maladjustment, and other maladies by the score right in the working mother's lap. But while mothers are being criticized and chastised for neglecting their children, fathers seem to be getting off scot-free.

Who decided that children are primarily the mother's responsibility? Most likely the men did. Men who had a bit of monopoly on delegating responsibility. And society at large has backed us up on this division of labor.

"Children are the mother's responsibility along with homemaking and housework," we've agreed all too easily. "And the man's responsibility? It's outside — safely outside — the home."

Appeals are occasionally made for fathers to squeeze out a bit of time for their children. Not because of the responsibility fatherhood includes, but out of the generosity of their souls.

"Spending time with their children is a privilege many fathers bypass simply because they refuse to take time from their already overly busy lives," writes one kind counselor. A privilege? Nonsense. It's a responsibility, and a responsibility second to none.

"If a dad fails to give generously from his overcrowded schedule, and to enjoy his family, and his children, someday he'll wake up to the fact that he's missed one of life's big bonuses." A son is a bonus? Wrong again. A son who is treated as a bonus soon senses it, rebels against it, and wins attention by the problems he creates.

After all, doesn't fatherhood carry with it a fifty-fifty debt to a child's future? A fifty-fifty share in a child's development? A fifty-fifty responsibility to a child's personal growth, personality and personhood?

∘ ∘ ∘

"Hey there, don't rush off, man." Jim's voice stops you as you swing tiredly into the car at a day's end.

"Gotta rush, Jim, it's gonna be a busy evening."

"Hey, I've been wanting to ask you about joining the bowling team we're getting up. We need you."

"I'd sure like to, but I'm working nights."

"Working nights? Anybody living in that nice new subdivision doesn't need two jobs."

"That's why I need it." (Your sentence trails; it's getting too close for comfort.) "I'd love to bowl with you guys, but it'll have to be out for now."

"OK, man, just don't kill yourself working."

"No danger. See ya!"

"No bowling," you say to yourself as you drive off. "Well, so what? I can do without it. It's the other things I'm missing more. No after supper playing catch with the kids. No evening at home. Except weekends. And last weekend it was like . . . like . . . when they'd gotten along without you all week, they could do without you for the weekend too. And no time to enjoy your new home. Just work to pay for it. By the time it's paid for it'll be too late for spending time with the kids. They'll be grown and gone. So they do without dad — when they need him — so he can pay for a better home than they need."

o   o   o

Has it come to your notice that fathers come up for mention in the Bible more often than do mothers? That parental responsibility is first laid on the man's shoulders? That the basic emphasis is on parents sharing parenthood share and share alike?

Note Paul's words to the Ephesian Christians:

Fathers, don't overcorrect your children or make it difficult for them to obey the commandment. Bring them up with Christian teaching in Christian discipline (Eph. 6:4).

Or to the Colossian Christians:

Wives, adapt yourselves to your husbands, that your marriage may be a Christian unity. Husbands, be sure you give your wives much love and sympathy; don't let bitterness or resentment spoil your marriage. As for you children, your duty is to obey your parents, for at your age this is one of the best things you can do to show your love for God. Fathers, don't overcorrect your children, or they will grow up feeling inferior and frustrated (Col. 3:18-21).

It is to fathers that the Bible gives its directives. It is to fathers that the final responsibility is given for shaping childhood into adulthood.

If this be so, then a father's time is not solely his own. If he chooses to become a parent, his time belongs to his wife and children as much as to him.

So what does a working man do — if he has chosen the primary responsibilities of marriage and parenthood? He lets them be primary! When he chooses his work, he lets his primary responsibilities actually come first.

117

There are business executives who have resigned their positions of power and finance because it kept them from being fathers and husbands to their families.

There are doctors, attorneys, educators, politicians, men from many professions who discovered that their work was crowding out their life as humans, as fathers, as family men — so they quit, or changed, or started over somewhere else.

They were men who set up their priorities in order of importance, who determined to be first of all a genuinely free person — a person with something to offer their families. Second, they determined to be a successful husband — a husband his wife can trust and count on to share a whole marriage. Third, they determined to be a father — a father who recognizes his responsibility in the formation of his children's lives, goals, and personalities. Where does this leave his job or his profession? In fourth place. He chooses it as a means toward the fulfillment of the other three goals. Namely — personal fulfillment, marital fulfillment, parental fulfillment. It does not become an end in itself.

o   o   o

"I'll get out here," you say to the other three guys in your car pool. "It's just a short walk through the park and I'm home. A little walking will loosen me up for bowling league tonight."

You swing your coat over your shoulder, loosen your tie, cut off through the trees . . . hey . . . this is great! You rub your grindstone-worn nose with an appreciative knuckle, drawing in the scent of honeysuckle. Then the low throaty laugh of a girl comes from beyond the bushes ahead.

"Hey, hey. The sounds of spring . . . spring on the make, no doubt." You slow your steps, not wanting to break in on anything unannounced.

There they are. Boy, girl, sunlight on the grass . . .

which arms belong to which? Couple of kids — 13, 14 — they're getting at this business younger all the time. The boy turns to nuzzle the girl's cheek. She lifts her face. In a flash of recognition the profile grabs you. Your stomach knots.

"Sheri!"

It can't be Sheri — not your girl. She's only a kid. She's not . . . she's not. . . .

But she is. It's Sheri, all right. The boy you've never seen before. And you look again at Sheri — like you've never seen her before either. Five minutes ago you'd have thought of her as a kid — bubble-gum-chewing girl, all elbows and ponytails. And here she is . . . lying in the grass with her head in some guy's lap.

You knew the girl Sheri. That was back before your promotion to department head. Then the responsibilities went to your head — or to the head of your schedule. And executive golf, executive travel, the executive social circuit tied up all your time. Now the young lady Sheri is a stranger to you. At this rate, she'll soon be a young girl gone to her own world — and what guidance have you given her? What values have you shown her? Or has she rushed into premature boy-girl relationships to gain the acceptance she's missed from you at home? And does she decide what to do with the boy in the park from the morals she saw in the last movie?

Will your schedule force her into an early marriage, too? Before she gets the chance to mature into a woman — emotionally, morally, educationally?

Can you let that happen? Or should you cut back on your schedule? Even take a step back in your career and shed a few of the time-consuming responsibilities?

o   o   o

Didn't God give children fathers for more than a chance

119

meeting at the end of the day? Are not parents meant to be patterns? A son's or daughter's values are caught from Mother and Dad. They cannot simply be taught by Mom and Dad. There must be first a gift of presence before there can be a gift of principles. Imitation is the means of maturing in the early years. Patterning is the process of first human growth.

o   o   o

Presence becomes even more crucial in adolescence. After a boy has found a model for identity in his father, he must break away to become his own man. Then he needs a father more than before.

> The trouble with today's young people in many cases is that they don't have anything to revolt against, no firm father whom they can use as a foil. It is crucial in every family that there be something to revolt *against*. I have a couple of sons, in college now, who are pretty healthy in their revolt against their parents' "archaic" views. I don't mind particularly, because I know the father's part in the process by which a young man tests himself, having first to find out what he is not before he can discover who he is. [30]

A young man cannot grow up in an environment of mush. He needs both encouragement and criticism, liberty and limitations. He needs the disciplines of living in close human relationships.

o   o   o

A father's presence is essential for a daughter, too. The close communication of a girl with her father provides a link for absorbing, testing, and forming her image of personhood.

"No one is born a woman, one is merely born a female. She becomes a woman," Simone de Beauvoir says in *The Second Sex*. [31]

Where, then, does a daughter find her model for femininity? In her mother? In part. And from her father's expectations, too; from both the mother's and the father's ideal image of what a woman should be.

Erik Erikson, the noted psychoanalyst, states that the child's identity is not modeled simply on the parent, but on the parent's "superego."[32] That is, on the parent's value system, ideals, and conscience.

So a daughter senses the parent's image of womanliness, and forges her own identity according to that pattern as she perceives it. If the mother-daughter relationship is fragmentary and superficial, then the self-image she puts together will lack depth and substantial character. If the father is absent, she will lack stability and a firm sense of character in relationship to the men in her life.

So the parent who says, "So what, it's just Susie (or Jimmy) calling, but she (he) can figure out whatever she (he) wants without my help," will someday overhear the son or daughter say, "So, who cares, that's just what the old lady (old man) says, but I don't need her (his) advice to live my life for myself!"

o   o   o

Parents who give presence, time, and attention to their children may then qualify to provide that elusive but all-essential quality called "discipline."

Discipline is not punishment.

"You can punish any child you have the right and strength to punish. You can only discipline those children who make themselves your disciples."[33]

It is the quality of life, love, and respect which the child senses in his parents that attracts him or repels him as he is choosing his patterns. Any parent can punish and reward a child. But only the parent who wins the child's respect truly disciplines.

Respect is earned, not commanded. Authority is only truly authority when it is recognized as such from beneath.

What goes together to make parents into disciplining people?

One: Consistency. Between teaching and practice of life, between expectations of the children and the applications of these identical demands upon themselves. Youth need and expect consistency even more than adults. Values will be ill-formed and personalities warped out of skew if inconsistency surrounds them.

Two: Respect. Respect for the dignity and the freedom of the child as a growing person. Where parents demand obedience for obedience sake, and submission to authority for its own sake, the end results tend to be negative and to create hostilities. Inconsistent authoritarian homes create tense and angry children. [14]

As A. Don Augsburger writes, "Authority and discipline are a means and not an end. Meaningful discipline understands and relates persons to truth in the context of loving concern." [15]

Effective Christian discipline is known by its quality, not quantity. It is not how much or how little discipline given that is the most crucial factor, but what kind of discipline.

Loving discipline is the Christian kind. The encouragement and correction of love. Loving concern. Concerned love. Love that gives itself unsparingly not to control, but to assist the child in maturing so that parental control becomes unnecessary.

Good parents work themselves out of the disciplining job as completely as possible. To free the child by instilling internal disciplines. Internal disciplines are the spine and skeleton of personal freedom. To voluntarily accept disciplines of life is to achieve true freedom. That is what parents hope to implant. By loving concern.

CHAPTER TEN

To Be Faithful in Forgiveness . . .

You pick the phone from its cradle, poke your finger at the first number, dial, and let it tick its way back. Your mind unwinds with it, sketching your plan of action. You'll call, you'll ask for your wife, you'll see if she's really at the club meeting as she said. Then you weaken. Sure you doubt her . . . but this is the first time your doubts have driven you to checking up on her.

You pause in the dialing, one digit to go. Is it that you want to quit and forget your fears?

Forget? Forget the strange distance that hangs between you? Forget her preoccupied moments that leave you feeling ignored . . . and even resented? Forget the occasional gaps in her schedule that stand unexplained? Forget the coolly automatic way she goes about everything from bedmaking to lovemaking?

How could there be any other reason? Unless it's you. Unless it's your suspicions building a wall between you.

You dial the last digit. The phone rings twice, then the answer. You ask for her by name . . . and wait. "Not here," is the reply. "But this is an emergency," you clip. "When did she leave? May I speak to someone who saw her go?"

"She hasn't been here," the reply comes back.

You sit holding the phone numbly. Now you've caught her in an apparent lie. Where could she be? Who would she be with?

The thought of her with someone else in some motel blinds you with blended fear and anger.

Or maybe there's a perfectly good reason — a flat tire, her carburetor's been acting up. How can you be sure?

What can you do? Wait until something big finally breaks . . . until she's seen with some guy, whoever he is? But how can you wait, suspecting her and beginning to suspect anybody or everybody, as you do? Should you do a little discreet inquiring from several of her friends who might know? But would they tell you if they knew? Or would word of your suspicions seep back all too soon?

Maybe you should hire a detective and gather the evidence to divorce her? Or should you confront her with your suspicions? Lay your conclusions right on the line? Then again, maybe if you showed her you really care, maybe she would tell you what's troubling her?

o   o   o

To be faithful to each other
   Begin with love.
   If love is taken for granted,
Continue with trust.
   If trust seems betrayed,
Go on with acceptance.
   If acceptance is undeserved,
Go all the way to forgiveness.
   Forgiveness is faithful love.

o   o   o

"Forgiveness is divine."
Especially when your wife asks
On your anniversary,
"Know what day it is?"
And you quickly reply,
"Sure, it's Tuesday."

o   o   o

"I always forgive," some claim. "I never refuse to forgive anyone."

"I never forgive anyone," others say. "Let them pay for their blunders."

The truth, for most of us, lies somewhere in between. All of us forgive — on occasion, in a fragmentary way. And all of us have refused in certain situations. Because it was just too much to ask. We couldn't bring ourselves to do it, not immediately.

Forgiveness is hard. Especially in a marriage tense with past troubles, tormented by fears of rejection and humiliation, and torn by suspicion and distrust.

Forgiveness hurts. Especially when it must be extended to a husband or wife who doesn't deserve it, who hasn't earned it, who may misuse it. It hurts to forgive.

Forgiveness costs. Especially in marriage when it means accepting instead of demanding repayment for the wrong done; where it means releasing the other instead of exacting revenge; where it means reaching out in love instead of relishing resentments. It costs to forgive.

o   o   o

SHE: "Sorry?" It'll take a lot more than a few "sorrys" to undo everything you've done to me.

HE: I can't undo the past, Mary, that isn't possible. What's done is done. But I would if I could.

125

SHE: So, after all you've put me through you expect to cover it all with an apology?

HE: That's all I have. . . . Will you forgive me?

SHE: I don't know if I can. Not yet. It'll take time.

HE: Time to see whether I keep my word?

SHE: Maybe.

HE: I'll have to prove myself, is that it?

SHE: Do you blame me for wanting a little evidence of change?

HE: I guess not, if you've decided I can't be trusted.

SHE: I'm not judging you. It's just . . . well, you ask for forgiveness like it was the easiest thing in the world. But forgiveness is hard.

HE: Why?

SHE: Why? Because I can't quit being angry just like that. (She snaps her fingers.) Not when I've carried these angry feelings as long as . . . well . . . it's been three years since I first began to suspect you were —

HE: Can't you forget all that?

SHE: Is that what forgiveness means to you — forgetting?

HE: Well, you know, "forgive and forget" they say.

SHE: I may be able to forgive, sometime. But forget it? God knows I wish I could. But it's part of me now. Always will be.

HE: So you can't forgive?

SHE: I didn't say that. I pray that I will. I just don't think forgiving and forgetting are the same thing.

HE: How do you mean?

SHE: Maybe I'll be able to forget my angry feelings, but I'll never be able to erase the memory of what happened.

HE: I guess no one could. But if the anger is gone, that's almost what forgiveness is, isn't it?

SHE: Maybe. I'll have to think about it. It's so hard.

∘   ∘   ∘

What is forgiveness? To answer, we must first agree what it is not.

Forgetting? Memory cannot be controlled at will. So many of the hurts we feel cut so deeply that the scar is permanent. They are not forgettable. When we have forgiven, we will be able to forget the anger we feel toward the person who harmed us, but the act itself will always be a part of our past. To forgive is not the same as to forget.

Pretending? No, forgiveness is not a dishonest game of pretense that says, "We'll just act as if it never happened." No amount of phony smiles or saccharine sweetness can turn the clock back. What is done is done. Forgiveness must accept the fact of the injurious act and reckon with it honestly.

Ignoring? No, forgiveness is not a game of "being big about it" and overlooking the hurt done. To overlook and ignore the hurt is to say, "It doesn't matter." "So what?" "It was nothing." Ignoring the hurt is a form of withdrawal. It is a way of dodging the real issues between us. It, too, is deceit.

o   o   o

What, then, is forgiveness?

Stated legally, forgiveness takes place when the injured party drops charges, cancels his suit for damages, and himself absorbs the loss incurred by the injurer.

When a man is wronged by another, either the party who was injured, the first party, forces the second party to pay. That is justice. Or else the first party accepts the injury done and sets the second party free. That is forgiveness.

Stated psychologically, forgiveness takes place when the person who was offended and justly angered by the offender bears his own anger, and lets the other go free.

Anger cannot be ignored, denied, or forgotten without doing treachery in hidden ways. It must be dealt with responsibly, honestly, in a decisive act of the will. Either the injured and justifiably angry person vents his feelings on the other in retaliation — (that is an attempt at achieving justice as accuser, judge, and hangman all in one) — or the injured person may choose to accept his angry feelings, bear the burden of them personally, find release through confession and prayer and set the other person free. That is forgiveness.

Stated practically, forgiveness takes place when the man hurt, smeared, betrayed, or cheated accepts the loss, and pays the cost of forgiving the other's wrongs, asking for no repayment, seeking no revenge, holding no resentment.

Repayment for most injuries is impossible. Revenge boomerangs on the revenger. Resentment sours the soul. Only forgiveness can bring healing and reconciliation. Forgiveness takes place when we say to the man who put us down, "You're OK with me again, fellow." Justice would say, "You're not OK, you pay." Forgiveness says, "God loves me, so I'm OK. He loves you, too. As far as I'm concerned, you're OK. We're OK."

Stated theologically, forgiveness, whether human or divine is essentially substitutional. It is vicarious. No man truly forgives his brother until he bears upon himself the hurt of the other's deed. God forgave us in Jesus because God was in Christ paying the cost of forgiving men by bearing the total hurt of our evil upon Himself at Calvary.

> Follow in His forgiving steps . . .
> He was unjustly assaulted;
>   He did not repay with insult.
> He was evilly abused;
>   He did not retaliate with threats.
> He trusted justice
>   To the One who judges justly.
> He accepted the cost of forgiving,
>   Carried all our sins with Him to execution,

He paid the cost of forgiveness in full.
So we are free through forgiveness
  If we accept it by ceasing our evil,
  If we receive it by living for righteousness.
He paid — in forgiving — the cost of our healing.
    (1 Pet. 2:21-24, *Author's paraphrase*)

God forgave us freely in Christ. He did not overlook sin, saying it did not matter. Calvary shows how much it mattered. He did not pretend or ignore the evil that we did and were. Calvary shows how deeply He involved Himself in our human tragedy. He paid the cost — the full cost — of forgiving.

Stated in marriage relationships, forgiveness takes place when love accepts — deliberately — the hurts and abrasions of life and drops all charges against the other person. Forgiveness is accepting the other when both of you know he or she has done something unacceptable.

Forgiveness is smiling silent love to your partner when the justifications for keeping an insult or injury alive are on the tip of your tongue, yet you swallow them. Not because you have to, to keep peace, but because you want to, to make peace.

Forgiveness is not acceptance given "on condition" that the other become acceptable. Forgiveness is given freely. Out of a keen awareness that the forgiver also has need of constant forgiveness, daily.

Forgiveness exercises God's strength to love and receive the other person without any assurance of complete restitution and making amends.

Forgiveness is a relationship between equals who recognize their deep need of each other, share and share alike. Each needs the other's forgiveness. Each needs the other's acceptance. Each needs the other.

And so, before God, each drops all charges, refuses all

self-justifications, and forgives. And forgives. Seventy times seven. As Jesus said:

> And when you stand praying, forgive anything you may have against anyone, so that your Father in heaven will forgive your sins. [If you do not forgive others, neither will your Father in heaven forgive your sins] (Mk. 11:25, 26) [36]

o   o   o

What is it that makes forgiveness so hard, so difficult for some that they refuse to forgive? And turn instead toward the twisted sicknesses of resentment, revenge, and the demand for repayment in kind?

Self-hatred can be a cause. Or an inability to accept love can render loving and giving love intolerable. To be forgiving, one must recognize that he, too, must be forgiven. To be loving, he must know that he is loved. To be capable of true forgiveness, he must experience the wholeness of love for others balanced by love for self.

o   o   o

To be forgiving, to be a forgiven person, calls for a wholesome measure of self-acceptance. Even self-love.

We don't often say that out loud. We get so tired of self-centeredness in others, so frustrated at it in our partners and in ourselves that any mention of self-love sounds treacherous. As selfishness always is. But to love yourself is not selfishness.

Self-love and selfishness are not identical; they are opposites. Selfishness is not love; it is a passion. Selfishness is a compulsion. Selfishness is an obsession.

Selfishness controls you, compels you, consumes you. It is dehumanizing and destructive. It isolates you, alienates you, makes marital intimacy impossible. It passionately idolizes self and self alone, centering its whole affections in the satisfaction of its desires and the meeting of its own

130

needs even at the expense of another. It gradually cuts itself off from relationships with others. It kills marriage. It will not forgive, because it cannot forgive. "Why should I forgive?" it asks. "There's nothing in it for me. It just lets the other guy off scot-free."

Self-love can be just as creative as selfishness is destructive.

Love for yourself is self-respect. You respect yourself responsibly for what you actually are, no more, and no less. (This frees you to respect others.)

Love for yourself is self-acceptance. You accept yourself in spite of what you have not yet become, not overlooking, not overpunishing. (This frees you to accept others.)

Love for yourself is thoughtful concern. You feel responsible, respectful concern about yourself and what you are and do, not overconcern that dominates your thoughts, not carelessness that abuses the self.

Love for yourself is a broad compassion that reaches out to include others. Unlike selfishness, which contradicts all other selves and competes with all other persons, love recognizes them as individuals and affirms that they are persons too, and practices forgiving and self-giving.

Erich Fromm, the psychologist who has written so helpfully on the experience of love for both self and others, notes:

> If it is a virtue to love my neighbor as a human being, it must be a virtue — and not a vice — to love myself, since I am a human being, too. . . . The idea expressed in the biblical 'Love thy neighbor as thyself' implies that respect for one's own integrity and uniqueness, love and understanding of one's self, cannot be separated from respect and love and understanding for another individual. The love for my own self is inseparably connected with the love of any other person. [37]

"You shall love your neighbor as yourself" (Mk. 12:31, RSV), Jesus commanded.

Christ did not say, "You shall love your neighbor better than you love yourself." Nor did He command, "Love your neighbor, and hate yourself." Or, "Love your neighbor to the loss of your own self and personhood."

"Love your neighbor as yourself," Christ said. And how flawlessly He loved both neighbor and self. He lived the perfect balance of love-for-neighbor, love-for-self.

But did He not teach us to deny — not love — ourselves?

No, the denial He taught was a denial of selfishness, of selfish attempts to guarantee our own safety and security in self-centered isolation. True love for self, as He commanded it, invests life wisely, unhesitatingly in a cause that is truly eternal. (See Mark 8:34-28.)

* * *

How will you live — if you, too, love yourself?

You will consider yourself as a person of worth and dignity. You are a person God recognizes, a person God loves. A person Christ chose to become like when He became a man, a person for whom Christ died. You are through birth a child of God — born in His image. You are through rebirth (I pray) a son of God — remade into His image through the Spirit of Christ. All this is reason for high self-respect, appreciation, and esteem. Christ calls persons to a high self-regard. This frees them to accept His forgiveness. They need not grovel in self-punishment. They are forgiven, freed.

It is selfish, self-centered brutality to punish yourself mercilessly for your own failures or shortcomings. Such unlove is no virtue, it is an illness. It follows the strange stages of: self-dissatisfaction to self-dislike, to self-pity, to self-punishment, to self-hatred, and eventual thoughts of self-destruction. Depression it may be called. It is self-hatred. Anger turned inward. A refusal to love and accept forgiveness for oneself.

Christ frees persons to give that identical respect to

others. Christ frees us to affirm the dignity, the value, the forgiven-ness of persons.

Husbands and wives can extend the identical high regard and affection to their mate. These two are indivisible. You cannot truly love and accept yourself without loving and forgiving your mate. You cannot truly love your partner if you do not love yourself.

If you can see this love-for-self-and-for-others as all of a piece, as one complete unity, it will free you to give love to others in a more selfless way. As it frees you to receive forgiveness without guilty self-punishment, it frees you to forgive, without needing to dish out your own brand of anger on others.

You will be able to love another as you love yourself; to respect another as you respect yourself; to forgive another as you want to be forgiven your own self.

○　○　○

when you love someone,
you love them as they are.
　not as you wish them to be,
　not as you hope to help them become,
　but as they are.

when you love someone,
you love them because they are they.
　not loving in order to change them,
　not loving as a way of remaking them,
　but loving because you love.

when you love someone,
you love them warts and all.
　not blinding yourself to their faults,
　not denying the other's imperfections,
　but loving in spite of. (God did.)

133

to love another
   is to commit oneself
   with no guarantee of return.

to love another
   is to give oneself
   with the risk of rejection.

to love another
   is to reach out in hope
   for our love to awaken love
   in the heart of the other.

love is not dependent —
   on the nature of the one loved,
   but on the nature of the one who loves.
love is not contingent —
   on the beauty of the loved,
   but on the appreciation of the lover.
love is not conditional —
   on the constancy of the beloved,
   but on the fidelity of he who loves.

when you love someone
   nothing matters half so much
   as to accept the other
   to reassure one another
   to hear and answer each other
   to look deeply into the other's soul
   and to show your own.

to love someone
   is to affirm that she is worthy
   to bid him live life freely
   to leave her with all her freedom intact

to recognize his dignity as a person
to invite her to grow
to oblige him to be fully what he is
to inspire her to become all she can be.

CHAPTER ELEVEN

Making Faith Real

Why do I need religion?
"To my grandfather, it may have been reality.
To my father it was a tradition.
To me it's a nuisance."
Religion, who needs it?

o   o   o

Why do I need religion?
I've got a mother who's forever preaching at me.
I've got a dad who is always laying down the law.
I've got a sister who's trying to reform me.
I've got a kid brother who lifts a weekly collection from my pockets.
What more do I need?

o   o   o

When a family's faith becomes only a religion and not a way of life, it dies. Dies with the generation that once possessed it. Parents neglect it, children reject it.

"Religion, who needs it?" they ask.

But then, where do they turn? Discard their parents' religion, and when they look again, they've found another. Man is and has always been inescapably and incurably religious. History demonstrates how difficult it is for anyone to remain nonreligious for long. Reject the last generation's religion and when you look again another has filled the vacuum. From a religion of ritual, rules, and rigorous legalism, a reacting person may swing to free thrillism, hedonism, just-for-the-kick-of-it-ism. But that too is religion. Or from the institutional anthill of religious activism a person may bounce to an escapism of apathy and uninvolvement. An isolationist religion.

Religion is natural. Inevitable. We all possess it, either secondhand on loan from others or firsthand as a do-it-yourself set of views and beliefs.

° ° °

Religion can be taught from one generation to the next. Faith is caught.

Fathers who are men of faith transmit their faith not as a body of facts to be learned, but as a contagion of love for God, which a son or daughter absorbs both aware and unaware. They have seen the Father in their father.

Mothers, whose faith spans generational gaps, are persons who consciously or unconsciously reflect the love, grace, forgiveness, and righteousness of God to their children. They have come to know God in her.

Faith and religion are totally different in kind.

Religion is man's self-constructed views and values.

Faith is a loving openness to Someone.

Religion is centered in a man: his own feelings, his own goodness, his own success, and his own piety.

Faith is simply being open — absolutely open — to God.

137

Religion

Religion is individualistic. The religious man is preoccupied with himself and forgetful of his neighbor. He may be a pious, puritanical perfectionist, but his religion revolves around himself and his own improvement.

Religion is man's effort. Defined as man's ultimate concern about life, or man's struggle for meaning, or man's search for God.

Religion is manageable. It is confined to one nice little area of life — usually an insignificant one.

Religion is self-centered. God is an accessory who may be called in if and as needed. Religion's God is comforting, always eager to rush to our rescue. He is one of us, our race, our nationality. A proper connection with Him makes us feel good, "for He's a jolly good fellow."

Faith

Faith is love of God, love of neighbor, love of self — in rightful priority, and yet all three bound together in an indivisible unity. Matthew 22:37. Faith is more like falling in love than like adopting a philosophy. It is falling into a love relationship with both God and man.

Faith recognizes that we cannot reach God, but we can respond to His reaching out to us in Jesus. Faith is humble openness to God who comes in seeking and saving love.

Faith commands all of a man's life. It lets God be Lord of every area in life — emotional, mental, moral, social, political.

Faith lets God be God. He alone is at the center of life to control, direct, correct, and strengthen. Faith is radical obedience to the God who expressed Himself to us in Jesus and radical acceptance of the Jesus way of life.

◦ ◦ ◦

SON: Dad, religion is nothing more than an odd assortment of prejudices, right?

DAD: I don't feel that way about it.

SON: I'm not saying you do. But look at Bill at church.

DAD: What about him?

SON: He's got a lot of prejudices, a lot of opinions, and a little religion all mixed up together.

138

DAD: Like what?

SON: Did you ever hear him talk about anything that he's for? It's all stuff that he's against.

DAD: Isn't that being a little hard on him?

SON: Not at all. Listen to him a little. Listen to the jokes he tells. He's against blacks, the Chinese, bingo, the communists, liquor by the drink, the Jews, pot, tobacco, and the Roman Catholics. And he's against them religiously.

DAD: (Chuckling) You have been listening to him all right.

SON: And you can laugh about it? He's an elder in your church.

DAD: Well, he's a decent sort of guy.

SON: Come on, Dad. That's not your definition of religion. All he's got is a load of prejudice.

DAD: And you think that's all there is to our religion — Mother's and mine?

SON: I didn't say that. I think it means something to you. But there are so many people in your set that turn me off. They're against everything. They think with their gallbladders or something.

DAD: I hope you've seen something more than that in our home. Something like faith.

SON: Sometimes I think maybe it's something real — this faith business, I mean. You have showed me that it's possible to live by what you believe.

o   o   o

Is it possible that *your* faith is only prejudice?

How could we know? Prejudice is always purblind to itself. The most prejudiced are least aware of it. Who of us knows his own prejudices? How could you sort out your prejudices from your opinions, from your convictions, from your beliefs?

How can you spot a prejudice and recognize it for what it is?

1. It's usually found lurking just behind a judgmental attitude, hiding behind a critical spirit. When you feel an unexplained urge to condemn another, there may be a prejudice behind it. When it's a conviction that's threatened, you can understand it, discuss it, and resolve it. But when it's a prejudice, it makes you critical, frustrated when in tension, and irritable when facing any conflict.

2. A prejudice may be detected as you feel anger's danger signals when you've been challenged. A quick difference between a conviction and a prejudice is that you can discuss a conviction without getting angry.

3. A prejudice may be discovered when you find no reason to explain your viewpoint except "you've always felt that way about it," or "you just feel that it's right or wrong," or "you just happen to feel. . . ."

What's wrong with this? Prejudices are liabilities! Prejudices are debits that are of no help at all when life begins to come up short.

You can't build your life on such empty skins of old bloated ideas. You need facts and faith. And if your facts are nothing but biased ideas bought at a bargain, if your faith is nothing but an accumulation of religious prejudices, you've no foundation, no structure, no stability to life.

o   o   o

Let's explore this in specifics.

Does your religious faith tend to make you critical of others? Do you find it easy to label, categorize, cubbyhole, and even condemn those who are not in agreement with you? Does your faith excel in cutting yourself off from others, more than in drawing others to you? Then it is not faith. It's a prejudice.

Does your religious faith tend to excite your anger when others disagree with you or disregard your ideas or insights? Do you find that religious discussions tend to leave you feeling negative, depressed, and down-in-the-mouth?

Then it's not much of a faith; it's more of a prejudice.

Do you find yourself at a loss when asked for even the simplest reasons for your faith? Do you easily slip over into attacking the other person's viewpoints rather than clearly sharing your own? Do you know what you don't believe much better than what you do believe? Then there is doubt if you have a faith. What you have is more likely a prejudice.

You see, faith is a positive matter. It is something you believe, something that you possess, something that you hold deliberately, honestly, decisively. A prejudice is something that possesses you, that holds you helpless in its grip, that masters and motivates your emotions and reactions regardless of your better knowledge.

Faith is an exercise of willed belief.

Faith is personal. An experience in trust.

Faith is voluntary. Or it is nothing.

Faith is a free choice. Or it is a farce.

Faith is a positive confession of truth that you know and trust.

Faith is love. It is a willful pledge of the heart and soul to all that it knows to be true and eternal.

Prejudice, by way of contrast, is something a man absorbs from his environment with no honest, open, candid basis in fact.

Prejudice is defensive. it is a position you back into. Its interest is self-preservation. Thus it collects negatives and accumulates distrusts and rejections.

Prejudice wraps itself in selfish safety and proud dreams of superiority. It is essentially comparative, incurably "better than."

You may be nudged into prejudice by the pressures of your environment. But faith is a personal choice. Faith is a decision to be free of prejudice, free to see things as they are.

Prejudice pushes men into pigeonholes, prejudges their lives and commitment. Prejudice draws deep lines that divide. But faith is a force that unites men in love. (See Ephesians 4:1-13.)

Prejudice is betrayed by a bent toward criticism, but faith is shown in how a man loves others and overlooks differences. (See James 2:14-26.)

Faith? Or prejudice? What have you?

.o   o   o

SON: You see, Dad? Can I help it if your generation's religion looks like a lot of "do's and don'ts" to us?

DAD: But that's only the way we worked it out — the specifics. You're not giving us credit for the real feelings behind it all.

SON: Are there any?

DAD: Of course, we had real meaning behind it.

SON: "*Had*," that's what you said. "We *had* real meaning." Don't you see? That's just what I've been saying.

DAD: And you think it's an empty book of rules to us?

SON: Well, I guess I do. When do you talk about love and concern for people? And when do you really hear each other?

DAD: Not often enough.

SON: I mean, your religion looks good on paper, but is that what Jesus was all about? So we could spell out a "Christianity" once and for all, and then have it down in black and white?

DAD: No. He gave us a way of life.

SON: That's the difference, isn't it? Some people like to spell it out and worship the paper, the creeds, the rights and wrongs, and all that. . . .

DAD: And some prefer to get on with living it.

SON: Right! It's like some people eat the menu . . . and others eat the meal.

o   o   o

Do you prefer the menu to the meal?

Parents fail to communicate a living faith when it comes off as paper ritual, not a personal reality. When faith is something they defend but fail to demonstrate.

It's all too easy to settle for a religious, public faith or even to know and quote orthodox statements of doctrine. But that is not a faith that survives more than a generation, unless it is a living, growing thing.

It is all too common for Christian parents to sing the praises of the Bible and yet never show that its truth grips and motivates their lives. They may even worship its words, but it only affects their child's future when it is clear that Mother or Dad knows how to live that Word. So no amount of defense for the Book will convince if parents fail to absorb it themselves and demonstrate it in life. Faith, like food, must be made fragrant in aroma and rich to the taste. And tasted daily.

Children know if parents stall with the menu and miss the meal.

Why tell the waiter, "Never mind the dinner; I'll feast my eyes on the menu card. I love the paper stock used, what tasteful layouts, what crisp type selections, what a rich use of languages — French, English, Italian. The menu will be all, thank you."

Who could be satisfied with print and pictures? Who can silence hunger by dreaming of the sensual delights of dining while reading food lists or salivating profusely over delicacies pictured in living color?

Some parents use their religious faith as an escape from the difficulties of life. Their real taste tooth is for pie-in-the-sky-by-and-by. But that doesn't seem to sweeten them now.

Are they now like the TV addict who prefers to live in a fantasy of soap operas rather than deal with the difficulties of her own life. Or the paperback reader who chooses to escape into the roles of yesterday's novel rather than pick up his own life and live it.

A faith that communicates is a faith that changes people now, that fills them with strength to love, that is satisfying their real needs.

Other parents will serve the cookbook, rare and without natural juices, in the vain hope that it may do for others what it cannot do in their own lives. But the child is soon wise to that. Even though the parents know the language, understand the recipes, praise the chef, and recommend the establishment, yet if they never taste for themselves, it's "no sale."

Why do parents stall when they realize what it costs to follow Christ? Why spout Christian truth, quote great Christians by the page, and cite commentators by the score, and yet not plunge personally into Christian living?

Why would a mother who fancies herself a great chef collect the best of cookbooks, memorize the choicest of recipes, and skill herself in name-dropping — of foods, menus, and desserts — and yet eat nothing but Rye-Krisp and water?

Perhaps they freeze when they realize that following Christ will demand their whole loyalty. In all of life. So they cover by majoring on some minor point but doing it in an all-consuming way. Or they crusade for this, campaign for that and yet never throw their whole souls into knowing Christ and following Him in life.

So they come off like a woman who fancies herself a great nutritionist, understanding all the intricacies of vitamins, carbohydrates, saturated/unsaturated fats — and yet is herself nothing more than a food faddist, falling prey to hucksters who sell her pressed hay and powdered birdseed, refusing to risk eating even a balanced meal.

Leave the menu. Go with the meal.

There is nothing that can be substituted. There are no alternative ways of knowing Christ or of sharing Christ. We must give Him loving attention. He's not known to be easily impressed. No amount of amassed knowledge seems to win Him over. Name-dropping doesn't seem to help.

He values friendship. Love. A relationship of acceptance, forgiveness, and the transparent honesty He tends to call repentance.

The parents who let Christ be "the secret center of [their] lives" (Col. 3:4) will succeed in transmitting that love to their children. It stands out. "Mom/Dad reminded me of Jesus," they will one day say. What more could any parent ask?

"Love Christ truly; follow Him daily in life." That's the entree to be noted on the menu. It's His RSVP request for your presence to share in the richest feast in life. He invites you.

His invitation is to friendship. Come for dinner. "Let Me satisfy your hunger for life, for love, for meaning," He offers. "Let Me quench your thirst for joy, for peace, for unending hope." That's how the invitation stands. You either take it — or make your excuses.

The dinner is ready.

The menu is in your hands.

Don't eat the menu!

CHAPTER TWELVE

Continuing Growth Together . . .

"How could I learn to know him better? We've known each other for two whole years! True, marriage will be different, but I know him now."

"He's just like I thought he'd be. Understanding, considerate, always loving. And we've been married one whole week."

"I can't understand how he could change so quickly. I thought I knew him better than this. But we just aren't getting through to each other now."

"I thought I knew him when we were married. But that was only the beginning of learning who he is. Now that the false faces are gone, I think I love him more."

o   o   o

DATING — the period of serious questioning when he or she asks, "Do I admire this person, do I love this person, do I want to be unconditionally loving to this person, more than to any other person I've known?" When the answer is "Yes," he or she is ready for betrothal.

ENGAGEMENT — the period of serious testing when he or she seeks to determine, "Can I live with this decision to love the other person unconditionally?" When the answer is "Yes," then marriage.

MARRIAGE — an unconditional commitment to love unreservedly, without opening the old dating issues again. Never asking, "Do I love this person as much as I might have X or Y? Could Z have made me more happy?"

Once a man or woman has accepted the involvement in the open unity we call marriage, he has little right to go back to the elementary questions of a beginning relationship.

Marriage — to be successful — is not a matter of finding the right person, but of choosing to be the right person. Forget whether you now have the perfect mate. You were for him/her when you made the selection. So what if you didn't find just the perfect-person-for-grand-old-you? The important consideration is: What kind of person are you willing to be?

o   o   o

"I take thee — as you are."

That's a nearly impossible commitment to expect of two people at the time of marriage. Neither knows the other person as he/she actually is. And to a large extent, never will.

"I take thee — no matter what I may discover you to be."

This is a possibility, in love. It accepts the other, recognizing that there will be times of tension when the other seems unacceptable. Yet love is willing to risk unfaltering

147

acceptance, to pledge love even when the other seems un-lovable. And in return to accept love, even when you know that you are not lovable.

Acceptance in marriage is the power to love someone and receive him in the very moment that we realize how far he falls short of our hopes. Acceptance in marriage is love among equals. It is love between two people who see clearly that they do not measure up to one another's dreams. Acceptance is loving the real person to whom one is married. Acceptance is giving up dreams for reality. [38]

o   o   o

Of all the poor jokes on newlyweds . . . like, "Reverend, you've got to do something about our marriage."

"What do you have in mind?"

"I wan't it, uh . . . an . . . annulled."

"Annulled? But that's impossible. Marriage is permanent, you know. And you took her for better or for worse."

"But that's just it. She's so much worse than I took her for."

Of all the poor jokes on newlyweds most of them turn on the frustrations of discovery (one) that the other person does not and cannot live up to all expectations and (two) that the other person is highly resistant to change.

Amazing, isn't it, how optimistic we are about remaking the one we love?

"It wouldn't matter to me what a girl looks like," a professional physical culturist once told me. "If she had good facial lines and the right personality, I could remake the rest in less than a year. You see, I could set her on the right diet and exercise program, and restyle her figure to meet any statistics I chose."

Surprising, how many young lovers conceal such designs on redesigning the personality of the bride-or-groom-to-be.

COUNSELOR: It's been a good evening of premarital counseling. You've been open. It's good. But I am
curious, Jim, no doubt you have several things
we didn't get to discuss. They're the things
you hope to change in Sharon. And I believe you, Sharon, have a few of these ideas,
too. Why not talk about them right now.
Start us off, Sharon. . . .

SHARON: Well, there are a few things. Little things, but
. . . I don't want to mention them.

JIM: No, go ahead.

SHARON: Well, it's the way you react when anyone
criticizes you. You sort of bristle, and quit
listening.

JIM: No, I don't I. . . .

SHARON: See, you get defensive so quickly. And I'd
like for you to be open to criticism, to want to
know what's wrong.

JIM: What else is there?

SHARON: Well, there's this funny way you laugh when
something goes wrong and you don't want to
apologize.

JIM: I always apologize, don't I? Oh, maybe I don't.
I guess it's pretty hard for me. What else?

SHARON: No, your turn.

JIM: Well, it gets me when you talk about us to
others, you know? I think everything about us
should be private.

SHARON: But I don't tell anything that matters. . . .

JIM: It matters to me. . . .

SHARON: OK go on.

JIM: Well, you're always so worried about how you
look. And you don't need to be. I wish you
wouldn't fuss so. . . .

COUNSELOR: That's about as far as we should go. . . .

JIM: Yeah? But how do I help her change?

COUNSELOR: You won't be able to.

JIM: What?

COUNSELOR: Sorry, perhaps I led you on. Understand, you are both going to change each other an awful lot in the first five years of marriage. But not likely on any of the things you just mentioned. Or on anything you set out to deliberately rework in the other. It doesn't work that way.

SHARON: Why not? I want to change if he doesn't like something I do.

COUNSELOR: Yes, now you do. But later on, change becomes threatening. When we try to remake the other, we're often saying to them — nonverbally — I'd love you more if you met my expectations.

JIM: You mean, we should love each other just as we are?

COUNSELOR: Isn't that how you want to be loved?

o   o   o

Is there anything in life that we humans resist more than change? Especially when it's not our idea, but the idea of someone we thought loves us for what we are?

Is it that we suspect their motives? Fearing that they want to recast us into their own image and likeness? Is it that we doubt their objectivity? Aren't we all much too close to our wife or husband to be able fairly to judge who should do the changing?

"To help another, is to give them the freedom to change." It is not helpful to attempt changing each other. That only arouses a person's defensive instincts, and puts him on guard against being engulfed.

It is not helpful to give unwanted and unrequested suggestions that point toward changes. That signals to the per-

150

son, "I would love you, if only. . . ." Or, "I'll love you more if you shape up to my expectations. . . ."

To be true to each other, we provide the freedom to change. That includes the freedom not to change as well. We've no choice but to accept that fact, and quit twisting our partner's arm.

What provides the freedom to change?

Love. Love that draws and attracts us to each other in genuine emotional-spiritual intimacy.

Trust. Trust that assures us we are not about to be remodeled if we open ourselves to each other, unhinging our armor, and coming out into the open with no defenses.

Confidence. Confidence extended to each other that inspires our own courage to face the shifting conditions of life, and adjust to their demands with flexibility.

Forgiveness. Forgiveness to accept the blunders we make and absorb the anger we would normally feel toward such acts.

Freedom. The freedom to change, feeling that we ourselves are the ones who may choose to change, voluntarily. Not out of the pressures of fear, but out of simple love.

Humility. Yes, humility is the end result. We come to recognize that it is the strength of God expressed within us through the Holy Spirit that is enabling us both to want — and to do — the changing that is constantly necessary. That is His work. To remake us into the image — not of each other — but of Christ. It happens bit by bit, as we are willing to open ourselves to His alterations within us.

As love and trust give us the confidence to venture openness, and forgiveness provides a context of freedom, we are able to humbly accept the strength of the Spirit to change and be changed. Not by each other, but together. By Him!

Be keener than ever to work out the salvation that God has

given you with a proper sense of awe and responsibility. For it is God who is at work within you, giving you the will and the power to achieve his purpose (Phil. 2:12b, 13).

°   °   °

HE: Imagine, twenty-five years! I never thought I could live with one face for that long, and not need a change.

SHE: It's good you said "face" and not figure.

HE: Well, that's undergone a lot of change, no problem of everything being unchanging there.

SHE: That's not the only way I've changed — weight, I mean.

HE: Oh, I don't know, you're still the same girl I married.

SHE: Am I? huh-uh! I've lost an awful lot of temper since those early years. Remember how angry I used to get?

HE: You were something else back there. But so was I.

SHE: You haven't changed like I have.

HE: That's what made me love you so much, all through the years.

SHE: What do you mean?

HE: You weren't impatient when I caught on slowly, and grew at a snail's pace.

SHE: I just happened to love you. What's special about that?

HE: The way you loved, that's what was special. I made blunders that could have ruined a marriage, with anyone who was slow to forgive. But you didn't let that happen. You let me try again.

SHE: You mean, the problem with the secretary?

HE: Why single out one? You forgave me more often than I knew.

SHE: What right would I have not to accept a few things and just get on with love?

HE: We're two different kids than we were when we said,

152

"I do," or was it, "I will?"

SHE: "I will." Yes, we are. But the changes are all for the good.

HE: I'll say. You know, I wouldn't want to be twenty again — I wouldn't want to be that blind and ignorant for all the tea in China.

SHE: You're a little hard on yourself, aren't you, honey? I wouldn't mind if you were twenty again tonight.

HE: You wouldn't?

SHE: Not if I were twenty with you!

o   o   o

Marriage is a covenant to mutual growth.

"We will grow together. Grow in tune with each other. Grow in openness each to the other."

"We will not seek to escape face-to-face relationships. We will look long into each other's souls."

"We will not seek to avoid life's problems. We will let them provide insights for more penetrating self-understandings."

"We will not eliminate our differences and individualities, but use them as opportunities for complementing the other's personality traits."

"We will accept the contrasts in our tastes, habits, opinions, prejudices, beliefs, and values as uncharted territory for mutual exploration and ongoing conversation, not as a battleground for intermittent conflicts."

Such marriage is a rich venture into relationship. As author-psychiatrist Dr. Paul Tournier writes:

In such an adventure, each partner in marriage develops. Each is able to go beyond the natural reflexes of his personality type and of his sex. There is a complete exchange. Each gives to the other the most precious dimension of his personality, and each gives the other that which was most missing. It is no

153

longer a question of masculine or feminine love, but of much more deeply human love in which each particular aspect of love is integrated. Finally, there is the sense of oneness which is not realized until they are sure that they no longer have anything hidden from each other. [39]

o   o   o

Marriage is a covenant of mutual growth to each person's fullest potential. Each of us possesses potentials which may lie fallow, unless love discovers them.

Each of us carries dormant possibilities that the other must arouse and release.

There is more to each one of us than the other ever sees. Depths that have not been plumbed. These must become known.

In marriage, the truly loving partner is one who constantly prays. . . .

"Holy Spirit, release every gift that lies dormant within my wife or husband. Fulfill every possibility. Let us not live out our lives without discovering the full potential You have entrusted to us. Give me the love that frees him/her to be all that he/she can be, through Your power."

o   o   o

I will give to you,
    A love that is patient.
    A love that is kind.
    A love that endures.

I will pledge to you
    A love that is not jealous, or possessive.
    A love that is not proud, or selfish.
    A love that is not rude, or inconsiderate.

My love for you
    Will not insist on its own way,
    Will not be irritable or resentful,
    Will not keep account of wrongs or failures.
        It will rejoice when good prevails.

Our love will know
    No limit to its endurance.

No end to its trust.
No fading of its hope.
  It will outlast everything.

Our love will stand
When all else has fallen.

Our life together
Will have three great qualities:
  Faith
  Hope
  Love
But the greatest is love. [40]

Footnotes

1 Editorial, *The Christian Century* (September 20, 1967), p. 1182.

2 I am indebted in this satire to Art Buchwald, "Problems of Being a Perfect Husband," *McCalls* (July 1963).

3 I am indebted here to John David Maguire, *The Dance of the Pilgrim* (New York: Associated Press, 1967), pp. 27-31.

4 Lois Gunden Clemens, *Woman Liberated* (Scottdale, Pa.: Herald Press, 1971), p. 35.

5 *Ibid.*, p. 36.

6 Ella May Miller, "The Liberated Woman" (Heart to Heart leaflet No. 644; Harrisonburg, Va.: *Heart to Heart*), p. 7.

7 Clemens, *op. cit.*, p. 61.

8 Letha Scanzoni, "Elevate Marriage to Partnership," *Eternity* Magazine (July 1968), p. 17.

9 Clemens, *op. cit.*, p. 47.

10 Albert Mehrabian, "Communication Without Words," *Psychology Today*, (September 1968), p. 53.

11 I am indebted here to a filmed lecture by Carl Rogers, "Some Learnings About Interpersonal Relationships," distributed by University of California, Extension Media Center, Berkeley.

12 John M. Drescher, *Meditations for the Newly Married* (Scottdale, Pa.: Herald Press, 1969), pp. 127, 128.

13 Dr. George R. Bach and Peter Wyden, *The Intimate Enemy* (New York: Avon Books, 1968), p. 122.

14 Dr. George R. Bach and Peter Wyden, *The Intimate Enemy* (New York: Avon Books, 1968), p. 27.

15 *Ibid.*, pp. 27, 28.

16 William C. Menninger, "Behind Many Flaws of Society . . ." *National Observer* (August 31, 1964), p. 18.

17 From *The Living Bible*, copyright © 1971 by Tyndale House Publishers, Wheaton, Ill. Used by permission.

18 Joseph C. Hough, Jr., "Rules and the Ethics of Sex," *The Christian Century* (January 29, 1969), p. 150.

19 Ella May Miller, "Sex Is a Sacrament" (Heart to Heart leaflet No. 657; Harrisonburg, Va.: *Heart to Heart*), p. 6.

20 David R. Mace, "Sex, Marriage and Maturity," *Faith at Work* Magazine, p. 7.

21 Jerry H. Gill, "Love and Sexuality," *Eternity* Magazine (September 1968), p. 11.

22 Quoted by Frederick Kirschenmann, "Sex Is for Play," *The Christian Century* (July 31, 1968) p. 966.

23 *Ibid.*, p. 967.

24 Quoted by William Luther White, *The Sacrament of Sex*, reprinted from *Together* (The Methodist Publishing House, November 1966), p. 4.

25 I am indebted here to Willard Claassen, *Learning to Lead* (Scottdale: Herald Press, 1963), p. 21.

26 Parable by James G. T. Fairfield, Radio Family Service Spots, January 1971, copyright Mennonite Broadcasts, Inc.

27 Ella May Miller, "Limit Your Budget" (Heart to Heart leaflet No. 658; Harrisonburg, Va.: *Heart to Heart*), pp. 6, 7.

28 Charlie W. Shedd, *Letters to Karen*, (Abingdon Press, 1965).

29 From *The Living Bible*, copyright © 1971 by Tyndale House Publishers, Wheaton, Ill. Used by permission.

30 Max Lerner, "The Vanishing American Father," *McCalls* (May 1965), McCall Corporation, New York.

31 Quoted by Harvey Cox, *The Secular City* (New York: Macmillan Co., 1966), p. 195.

32 Erik Erikson, *Identity and the Life Cycle* (New York: International University Press, 1959).

33 Ernest M. Ligon, *Dimensions of Character* (New York: The Macmillan Co., 1956), p. 447.

34 A. Don Augsburger, *Creating Christian Personality* (Scottdale: Herald Press, 1966), I am indebted here to pages 62-65.

35 *Ibid.*, p. 66.

36 From *Good News for Modern Man* (TEV). Copyright © by American Bible Society, 1966, 1971. Used by permission.

37 Erich Fromm, *The Art of Loving* (New York: Harper & Row, 1956), pp. 58, 59.

38 Gibson Winter, *Love in Conflict* (Garden City, New York: Dolphin Books, 1958), p. 115.

39 Paul Tournier, *To Understand Each Other*, John Knox Press, Richmond, Va. (M. E. Bratcher, 1967).

40 Paraphrased from 1 Corinthians 13:4-8, 13, RSV, and J. B. Phillips translations.

THE AUTHOR

David Augsburger is a forceful writer and speaker with a compassionate heart for the needs of people. He recommends marriage from his experiences with Nancy, his wife, and their two daughters, Deborah and Judith.

With a PhD in pastoral psychotherapy and family therapy from the School of Theology at Claremont, California, he is now professor of pastoral care at the Associated Mennonite Seminaries at Elkhart, Indiana. He received his BD degree from Eastern Mennonite Seminary, Harrisonburg, Virginia.

He served two pastorates and for many years was speaker for the Mennonite Church's radio release, *The Mennonite Hour.* In addition to his books he has written hundreds of magazine articles as well as award winning scripts for radio and television on family and peacemaking themes.